MAKING SENSE OF THE MEDIA

MAKING SENSE OF THE MEDIA

A Handbook of Popular Education Techniques

ELEONORA CASTAÑO FERREIRA
AND JOÃO CASTAÑO FERREIRA

MONTHLY REVIEW PRESS
NEW YORK

Library of Congress Cataloging-in-Publication Data
Ferreira, Eleonora Castaño
    Making sense of the media : a handbook of popular education techniques /
by Eleonora Castaño Ferreira and João Castaño Ferreira.

        p.   cm.
    Includes bibliographic references.
    ISBN 0-85345-880-4 : $17.00
    I. Mass media—Study and teaching—Handbooks, manuals, etc.
I. Ferreira, Joao Paulo Castaño. II.Title.
P91.3.F4 1993   94-11818
320.23'07—dc20   CIP

Monthly Review Press
122 West 27th Street
New York NY 10001

Manufactured in the United States of America

10 9 8 7 6 5 4 3 2 1

CONTENTS

INTRODUCTION BY TRACY GROSS   7

PART 1:   EDUCATION FOR LIBERATION   15

PART 2:   WHAT POPULAR EDUCATION IS ... AND ISN'T   25

PART 3:   A CURRICULUM FOR MAKING SENSE OF THE MEDIA   47

PART 4:   POPULAR COMMUNICATION   71

PART 5:   POPULAR EDUCATION AND MULTICULTURALISM   119

Introduction by Tracy Gross

In 1993, Eleonora and João Paulo Castaño Ferreira, Brazilian educators working in New York City, came up with the idea of using popular education techniques to demystify the influence of the mass media. After years of teaching in adult classes initiated by inner-city union education departments, they found that media domination was one of the biggest obstacles to the development of critical thinking both inside and outside the classroom. The result is this curriculum, *Making Sense of the Media*.

This workbook is designed to bring the principles of popular education to North American classrooms. My own introduction to popular education came in 1986 when I was working as program director for United Auto Workers Local 259 in New York City. I was involved in a small program for immigrant workers in an electronics factory. In 1989 I joined the International Ladies Garment Workers Union (ILGWU) to be director of their English as a Second Language (ESL) adult education program. I saw these programs addressing two problems: organizing workers who were without a union and advancing the potential for organized workers to advocate for themselves at work, in the union, and in other areas of society.

Both programs were sponsored by the Consortium for Worker Education (CWE). The consortium was founded in 1985 by a group of seven New York City unions under the leadership of Teamsters Local 237 and its education and training director, Joe McDermott. The group provided funding for union education programs while allow-

Workers in the Teamsters' Union using puppets in ESL classes.

ing autonomy for each union to create and administer its own program to best suit the needs of its particular membership. Paulo Freire was the keynote speaker at one of the first conferences sponsored by the CWE.

For many years Freire has been recognized as the foremost thinker and practitioner of popular education. His work has been interpreted in various ways—the books and articles purporting to develop Freirean ideas, especially attempts to adapt them from their original third world setting to Europe and North America, could fill a small library. However, because we tend to eliminate or talk around the political context of our situations, there has been a strong tendency to dwell on reflective discussion in the classroom at the expense of action. This has kept projects using popular eduction techniques from realizing their potential. The approach used in this book tries to correct this misapplication of popular education methodology.

How useful is the popular education approach in union education, specifically in an English as a Second Language program?

Learning the language is a way to enter into the society. It is the key to the culture. How it is learned can determine, or at least strongly influence, the social role an immigrant will assume.

My observation and experience is that new immigrants have an unusually complex uneasiness about entering and actively participating in the new society, despite their strong desire to do so. Conversations with students, teachers, and union staff with similar experiences confirm this. They describe having to let go, or hide, a big part of themselves and assume another or other personalities that they are not very comfortable with. In the traditional ESL classroom, very little of students' "learned" behavior in expressing themselves in English transfers from the classroom to the "real world." In fact, many students with this kind of learning never use English *except* in the classroom.

In contrast, where popular education methodology has been implemented consistently, I've seen workers, both quiet and extroverted, move into new situations with confidence. Something different is operating there, especially with students who have been active in the program. Often they have learned more English in such organizing activities as student council meetings than in the classroom. In university conferences or orientations and in meetings with teachers or union leaders or academics, I have seen students with a strong base in popular education naturally assume their participation has validity; their opinions and input do not necessarily have to conform to others but can stand on their own. For example, one group of students at an orientation, when asked to give "the students' point of view," formed a circle, getting input from each member of the group, prioritizing, reaching consensus and reporting back a collective opinion, without repeatedly using the same spokesperson.

This process was never "learned" or discussed as a technique, unlike the "five steps toward assertive behavior," or "communication skills building," or the most common union course, "leadership skills." It is an expression of a way of being in a learning/acting situation. There is no line between the class and life if the methodology is followed well and consistently. I believe the behavior I describe is evidence of the "subject vs. object" condition Freire describes as the basis of this education.

Most recent union education contrasts with the traditional organizing model: it is specialized, with separate courses taught by "experts" from community colleges, labor education departments of universities, or consulting organizations. The three main areas are technical training, basic education (such as ESL), and labor education focusing on shop steward and leadership training. The latter mostly emphasizes learning "skills" such as public speaking, communication skills, how to run a meeting, etc., outside of the context of work/union problems. This prevents workers from making connections to the larger issues affecting them and from reflecting on the bigger picture in which the dynamics of the power relationships play out. Here is where popular education technology begins to break the boundaries of traditional adult education.

My three years with the Local 259 project served as a starting point for my break from typical union staff assumptions. For most of this time I worked with an excellent ESL teacher, Laura Gothowitz, who had pre-

viously taught in Latin America and was herself learning the basics of the popular education approach. Eager to start some internal organizing within the ESL program, I was attracted to the emphasis on using relevant content in the curriculum, subjects that reflected the lives of the workers, most of whom were women. I thought that after some preliminary work we could begin to use contracts and other union materials, and that by talking about issues important at the time—city elections, solidarity with other union workers, etc.—we could start getting people politically active on their own behalf within the union.

I soon discovered that I was not sufficiently sensitive to the educational needs of the students, to their history in the union, or to their experience as immigrants and women workers in general. This was brought home to me when I asked one of the women in the class what her goals were, what she wanted to do in the future. She began to cry—she said no one had asked her that before. This experience made me stop and rethink what I was doing. I started to listen more and stopped looking for results based on my own expectations. Laura and I began to work on a slow process that combined speaking, reading, and writing English in the context of everyday work problems, discussions about early learning experiences, the students' first work experiences in this country, problems attending class, their family life here and in their own countries.

In their two-to-three years of experience in the class, the students created several booklets, including a collection of oral histories about their shop and a book of poems and stories about their relationships with their mothers. They developed a small community through the program and as a group solved some communication problems with their supervisor. The shop floor dialogue was brought into the classroom, where students studied it, role-played it, and discussed and role-played new strategies, eventually trying them out on the shop floor.

The key turning point came when the students had to make a decision that would affect the future of the class. When Laura, their teacher, had to leave her position, the women were very upset and talked of quitting the program. For some of them Laura and the class had been their only positive learning experience. We talked about this and eventually agreed that the selection of a new teacher had to be a group decision. The students interviewed applicants and voted on who should be hired. This experience seemed to be consistent with the methodology we were trying to follow.

My initial goals of internal organizing—students moving into activist roles in the union, becoming more involved in the political activities of the union—were not realized. But the students did become activists inside the program and had used some of their skills to advocate for themselves in the workplace. We began to discuss how these experiences could be built upon and expanded to create a bridge into the larger arena of union leadership or community action.

When I moved to the ILGWU, I was able to look at the program as a whole, rather than just the classroom, in terms of the methodology. The ILGWU program offered favorable conditions for developing an organizing model of education. For one thing, students were recent immigrants from Asia, South America, Central America, and the Caribbean. Having already taken serious risks in coming to the United States, they were not afraid to act.

In addition, the ILGWU had an early history of union education that reflected goals and processes that were similar to

Workers in the International Ladies Garment Workers Union (ILGWU) using puppets in ESL classes.

the model we wanted to create. It was one of the first unions to establish its own education program, shortly after it was organized in New York City in the early 1900s. The education program was geared to prepare recently organized workers for their role in building the union and participating in the labor movement generally. The curriculum combined language learning with instruction in economics, history, public speaking, and literature. It was run by union staff and educators from the academic community, with a decentralized structure that allowed autonomy for the locals. These parallels—in structure, staff, and curriculum—to the present adult ESL program seem to reflect a common goal: to foster organizing (questioning and acting) and the development of what we called an "organizing consciousness."

Another aspect of the ILGWU's history made it a good place to try such a project: it was originally built on a base of newly organized immigrant women workers. The present program was also made up of new immigrants, also mostly women, who were working to build a new life for themselves and their families. While today industry jobs are going to low wage countries, there is an increase in sweatshops in the United States, where the conditions are similar to those in the factories at the beginning of the century. In this context, much of the concrete experience described in this book took place.

I met Eleonora and João Castaño in 1991 when they visited an ILGWU workshop on the global economy. They felt at home and participated easily with the staff and students from our union's adult education program. From their experience working in the *favelas* (slums) of Río, they brought

a strong organizing perspective to the discussion. They supported the popular education approach that the teachers—Maureen LaMar, Emily Schnee, and myself—had developed for the workshop, one that started with a personal connection to the globalization of the garment industry: looking at the labels in our clothes, and later exploring the connection between the movement of the industry and the direction of the union's organizing efforts. Eleonora and João identified with the goal of our work, which was to bring about a discussion of the possibilities for international solidarity among workers.

It was clear that everything about their use and understanding of popular education methodology came from a strong conviction about its political intent. This was my first contact with practitioners who were committed to the methodology because they wanted to bring about social change *and* to speak about the options for action that are realized by this approach. For them, anything short of this was *not* popular education but what are generally referred to as "participatory" teaching techniques.

In adult ESL classes it is not unusual for instructors, trying to implement popular education methodology, to get stuck in the analytical, reflective stage of the process. I have found that this problem comes from an all-too-common strongly academic orientation to the practice, which is supported by a cultural context of individualism. In this country, individuals are expected to solve all their own problems themselves, and the sources of problems are seen as psychological in origin. Solutions to problems are sought through "talking them out" in "sensitive" groups. In classrooms, it is common to analyze, reflect, and re-analyze, denying the influence of political and economic factors on our personal conditions, or assuming that we have no power over these larger factors. Working with the Castaños and traveling to Brazil in 1992 with a group of labor educators strengthened my view of the need to go beyond the academic emphasis of most of the work in the field of adult education.

In popular education practice, the step of making connections from the personal to the broader context needs a lot of attention and support from program developers. In a union program it is critical. For unorganized garment workers at a Brooklyn ILGWU program site, who have known discrimination and bad working conditions, the first lesson was that they were not alone in their problems. Secondly, they learned their rights, how to file for back pay, and how to get the union to advocate for them. Their own action was to create a skit showing how workers could collectively and assertively respond to these problems; the skit was always well-received by students. The next year, the union coordinators began applying the popular education approach to their organizing workshops at the site. Students then quickly defined an action response appropriate to their needs and context.

Outside the classroom, much is written and discussed about the need for workers in manufacturing to participate more in decision-making related to production, particularly where production is affected by restructuring or new technologies. Workers and unions need to be ready to advocate for their rights in this situation and often have to negotiate new job descriptions, schedules, rates, etc., as well as suggest alternative strategies for production design and management organization that does not eliminate or downgrade jobs. Education in these situations involves new production processes, new communication and technical skills, and sometimes basic education.

In this situation, union staff and members can be easily co-opted into management schemes if critical thinking is not present at every stage. Companies are sophisticated in the use of language and training techniques derived from simplifications of popular education and adult learner practices. Although they seem to project an enlightened perspective, not much is offered that benefits workers.

Earlier I wrote briefly about my own learning experiences when first starting to work with the methodology—the breakdown of my assumptions and the letting go of the desire to control outcomes. This process is ongoing. Being able to allow outcomes to evolve from the starting point of the participants' perspective, eliciting input from many points of view, takes skill and trust. But the practice also builds trust. This practice, employed in other union situations, could help us develop better support for each other as well as develop stronger resources, ideas, and energy for all projects.

These experiences with popular education techniques offer a challenge to develop internal organizing in the unions, with a renewed emphasis on teamwork between union representatives and workers. But most important is determining how new skills are used, how accountability is to be guaranteed, how the system of communication is created and maintained, and how to approach problems like compensation or the integration of different work areas. Workers need to take the lead in these determinations, as only they know the reality of the work and the organization of production. Popular education techniques are a unique vehicle for realizing this goal.

✳ ✳ ✳

Eleonora Castaño Ferreira died of vasculitis at age 55 in May 1996, as this book was entering its last stage of production. Though she had been ill for months, the end of an exceptional life came suddenly and broke many hearts.

A proud Brazilian, Eleonora had made New York City her home, and the city's working people became her cause. With her years of experience as a popular educator in Rio, she could have easily found a niche in academia. But she chose instead to go where the action was, where people were trying to use popular education to help workers master their situations. She went first to unions and community organizations, reaching out to people in these settings, influencing many in a short period of time.

From New York, she went anywhere in the country where her popular education workshops were sought: a small college in Maine, a workers' organization in California, Columbia University Teachers' College, a public school in the Bronx. Wherever she taught, she emphasized that education had to be practical: it had to deal directly with peoples' realities and their root causes.

Her approach was consistent in all contexts, and she was the same person wherever she went. The status of individuals and organizations was not important to her. She was committed to the long term: her work in Brazil, and perhaps Brazilian culture itself, prepared her for this. Disappointments and defeats that would discourage us, her U.S. collaborators, did not faze her. She would laugh them off and get on with what she knew needed to be done. Her interest in the U.S. union movement reflected this outlook—neither cynical nor naive, she saw every development as part of a long process unfolding.

Her friends would get frequent phone calls with news from Brazil, which always brought forth insights into our ongoing work here. She was optimistic, generous, and committed without a backward step. She is greatly missed by those who were fortunate enough to have known her.

Part 1

EDUCATION FOR LIBERATION

Popular education is more than a new approach to teaching. It's a means to an end: the empowerment of powerless groups through their own experience—by becoming conscious of, and working to change their own social conditions.

In popular education the participants are educators and learners, not teachers and students. The learners are the SUBJECT, an active force, and not the OBJECT—the passive "product" of the educator's work.

The techniques of "education for liberation" were born in the third world—in Brazil, to be exact—in response to the specific forms of oppression that poor people in that country face in their daily lives. Over the years, popular education as set out by Paulo Freire, a Brazilian educator, has spread to other countries in Latin America, Africa, Asia . . . and more recently, to the inner cities in the United States.

Popular education stresses learning by going to the roots, analyzing the particular historical circumstances of a given situation. The same method applies in understanding popular education itself.

In the last forty years, the Latin American countries have passed through tremendous socioeconomic, political, and cultural upheavals. Military dictatorships rose and fell, dependent economic models became more dependent; revolutionary movements

exploded, and sometimes won victories. The process of industrialization grew in many countries, mainly in Brazil, the biggest and richest country in Latin America.

In the 1980s, the crisis of the foreign debt and other international problems paralyzed the economic development of almost all Latin American countries. Poverty, massive unemployment, the destruction of public services, and crime grew and menaced the people as never before.

The process of industrialization, controlled by multinational corporations, brought about another form of control: *cultural domination*. The traditional culture of Latin America, with a strong influence of the Indian and African peoples, began to be crushed by the mass-produced culture of the first world countries. The new set of values transmitted by the mass media, mainly *consumerism*, began to be absorbed by the Latino people.

In this context, among these people, popular education became a widely practiced, influential force.

THE STARTING POINTS

It was born in Brazil in the late 1950s and early 1960s, during a period of political reform. All the struggles and contradictions connected to industrialization were especially strong in Brazil.

In its enormous territory (8.5 million square kilometers) are widely different regions, from the Amazon rainforest with a population of Indians, rubber-tappers, nut-pickers and miners, to the cultivated plains of the South with small farmers descended from Germans and Italians; the Northeast region, stricken by poverty and drought for the last three centuries; the rich developed Southeast, the industrial and financial center of Latin America; the immense plains of the middle west, with rainforests, the gigantic swamps of Mato Grosso, and huge cattle and grain farms. The 150 million Brazilian people, a mixture of races and cultural traditions, are remarkably creative and versatile.

There, as elsewhere, the 1960s was a time of great political activity, particularly among religious youth. Young Catholics were inspired by the relative openness of the government of the time, and by progressive changes in church doctrine brought on by Pope John XXIII. They were more open to new ideas and approaches to working for social change than the traditional political parties.

One of the most active movements was the Catholic Action group, made up mainly of Catholic University students and the Young Catholic Workers organization. Catholic Action developed a uniquely efficient method of analysis to understand their reality, and action to transform this reality. Their method was based on three steps: *Ver*—TO SEE, *Julgar*—TO JUDGE, *Agir*—TO ACT.

In practice, this meant: (1) TO SEE the situation lived by the participants; (2) TO JUDGE (or to analyze) this situation at its root causes, including its particular socio-economic, political, cultural aspects; (3) TO ACT, to change this situation, following the precepts of social justice.

The members of Catholic Action were organized in small groups. At weekly meetings, they used the method to analyze their immediate situation and plan action in workplaces, in the universities, in the neighborhoods, in political parties, in

POPULAR EDUCATION: THE METHODOLOGY
A SET OF POLITICAL AND PEDAGOGIC PRINCIPLES TO USE IN THE PROCESS OF PRODUCTION OF KNOWLEDGE

POLITICAL PRINCIPLES

- The first principle of popular education is the need to democratize power relationships in our society.

- The means to this end is the creation of mechanisms of collective power over all the structures of society.

- The methods used in creating these mechanisms cannot be in contradiction with the first principle—a democratic society cannot be built through authoritarian methods.

- Popular education is a political process in which the projects, strategies, and tactics used are produced collectively by the participants themselves.

PEDAGOGIC PRINCIPLES

- The learners are the SUBJECT, not the OBJECT of the learning process, and through this approach they can become the subject of society.

- The educators and the learners are equal participants in the learning process—all are the producers of knowledge. The learning process is developed through a continuous dialogue between the educators and the learners.

- The objective of the learning process is to liberate the participants from the social pressures and internalized ideas that hold them passive in conditions of oppression—to make them capable of changing their reality, their lives, and the society they live in.

unions, etc. Many members of Catholic Action went to work among the illiterate workers of Brazil, teaching them to read and write and to organize themselves to take an active role in the country's destiny.

Enter Paulo Freire. He began a literacy program for peasants and shantytown dwellers in the 1950s and 1960s. His first program, *Movimento de Cultura Popular* (MCP) was sponsored by his home town Recife in northeastern Brazil. In the MCP Freire first developed his educational methodology. In 1961 the Catholic Church sponsored a national literacy program, the

Movimento de Educação de Base (MEB). The MEB was modeled on the MCP, but went further to incorporate worker organization and action. Finally, in 1963, Freire was asked by Brazil's Ministry of Education and Culture to coordinate a national literacy campaign.

His group of coworkers came from Catholic Action, the University Students' Associations, and other organizations that had great influence in the political activism of that period.

This group of educators set for themselves a double task: to develop an efficient

FAVELA

FA VE LA

FA VA LA

FE VE LE

FI VI LI

FO VO LO

FU VU LU

NEW WORDS:

VALA	(drain)
FAVA	(pod)
VELA	(candle)
LUVA	(glove)
FILA	(line)
VILA	(village)
VIVO	(alive)
FULO	(angry)
LEVA	(carry)
FALA	(speaks)
VOVO	(grandfather)
FIVELA	(buckle)
FALAVA	(spoken)
LEVAVA	(carried)
LAVAVA	(washed)
VELAVA	(awakened)

literacy method for adults, and to raise the social consciousness of Brazilian workers. They found out that the workers were resigned to their situation in society, that they thought that it was impossible for them to change this situation.

In their experience with the workers, Paulo Freire and his group of educators used the Catholic Action method—TO SEE, TO JUDGE, TO ACT—and discovered that when people began to talk about their problems in a community, and began to plan some action in response to these problems, they began to free themselves from their fatalism, their internal oppression.

The educators also discovered that the most efficient literacy method was the use of *generative words and themes,* words and themes drawn from the life experiences of the learners.

The educators developed the technique of dividing a generative word—for example, "FAVELA" (shantytown)—into syllables and presenting variations on these syllables by changing the vowels. The learners memorized the various "chunks of words" and put them together, forming new words and demystifying language (below).

The next day, the educators used a second chart with another generative word taken

NEW WORDS:

JA	(immediately)
TE	(the letter T)
LOTO	(lotto)
LOJA	(shop)
TOLO	(fool)
LUTA	(fight)
LATA	(can)
LAJE	(cement slab)
JOTA	(the letter J)
JATO	(jet)
TETA	(udder)
TELA	(picture, screen, canvas)
JILO	(a type of fruit)
LATE	(it barks)
LAJOTA	(small flagstone)
TITULO	(document)

TIJOLO

TI	JO	LO
TA	JA	LA
TE	JE	LE
TI	JI	LI
TO	JO	LO
TU	JU	LU

from the previous discussion: "TIJOLO" (brick). Once again, the learners used chunks of words to make new words.

After that exercise, the learners combined chunks of words from the two charts to create more new words.

This method can be used with phonetic languages like Portuguese, Spanish, and Italian. With English we have to develop other methods using whole words— words with similar sounds, etc. But the principle is the same: to use generative words/themes drawn from the reality lived by the learners.

From this practice was born the theory known as the Paulo Freire methodology. Freire formulated a set of political and pedagogical principles that systematize the methods, techniques, strategies, and goals of popular education.

The principal goal of the Freire methodology is to enable learners to transform themselves from passive objects to active subjects in social life and struggles. The educator and the learners are equal participants in the learning process. The process is developed by a continuous dialogue between the educator and the learners: it is a *dialogical* methodology.

The national literacy program directed by Paulo Freire met with great success, but it was of short duration. After a military coup in 1964, Freire's co-workers were arrested and persecuted; many were forced to flee Brazil, and all their work was declared subversive and destroyed.

While he was a political exile in Chile at the end of the 1960s, Freire wrote his famous book *Pedagogy of the Oppressed* (published in the USA in 1971). In this and in his other books, Freire developed the theory of his practice as a popular educator. These books are about the philosophy of his work, about the concepts, the general directives, not about the practice, the lessons, the activities in the classroom.

Why? Because each practical experience with each group of learners is different from the others. Each educator has to develop his or her own techniques, lessons, etc., with his learners, for each group's reality is different from the others.

There are no ready-made formulas for applying the Freire methodology in a classroom, and this is perhaps the biggest difficulty for many educators. They have to free themselves from the traditional concepts of the educational process where the educator is the sole source of knowledge and the students are only receptors of this knowledge.

And the only way educators can learn this is through practice: they have to *practice* the Freire methodology in order to learn it. Theory and practice are inseparable: from the practice is born the theory, and the theory refers back to the practice to be changed and reformulated. In short, **THEORY IS A MOMENT OF PRACTICE.**

PRACTICAL APPLICATIONS

In the last twenty years, popular education developed enormously in Brazil, in the grassroots organizations like the Christian Base Communities, trade unions, the landless peasants movement, and neighborhood associations.

Popular educators were also activists. In

the progressive movements in Brazil, education is not separated from organization and political or social action; they are recognized as dimensions of the same process.

In their practice in the different organizations, popular educators developed new methods, techniques, teaching tools, according to the different circumstances of each moment. The many different socioeconomic, political, and cultural conditions existing in Brazil's vast territory produced an incredibly rich variety of popular educational experiences that are always changing, always regenerating.

Through the decades, as popular education spread throughout Brazil, working people have used its techniques in the organization of new trade unions in the cities and in the countryside. These unions were militant, fighting the old union system subordinated to the Ministry of Labor.

In 1979, representatives of trade unions, Christian Base Communities, and grassroots organizations from all over Brazil founded the Workers' Party (*Partido dos Trabalhadores*—PT). Popular education had a significant hand in the growth of all these organizations from which the Workers' Party emerged.

In 1983 the independent unions founded the Unified Workers' Center (*Central Unica dos Trabalhadores*—CUT), the first labor confederation organized (without "authorization") during the military dictatorship.

Today the CUT has five national schools of popular education, where labor educators/organizers from all over Brazil take on courses developed according to the needs of the movement in all regions of the country.

The CUT has a National Education Sec-retariat that coordinates the National Plan of Education, and State Education Secretariats that coordinate the education programs at the state level. Each union has its own local education department for the rank-and-file members with programs designed to meet the needs of the movement at the local level.

The PT also has a National School of Popular Education, a National Education Secretariat, State Secretariats, and permanent courses at all levels, developed according to the needs of the national and local situations.

University professors, economists, and other intellectuals connected with the PT collaborate in these courses. They provide extensive research and data about important national and international socioeconomic, political, and cultural issues. This work is considered indispensable for developing the party's projects, strategies and tactics.

While this Brazilian experience can be useful to educators of other countries, we have to keep in mind the central concept of "education for liberation": theory and practice are inseparable. From different practices in different socioeconomic, political, and cultural contexts, are born different theories—the formulation of these practices.

Educators who want to practice popular education have to use the experience of earlier popular educators. Like Paulo Freire and that first group of educators who went to work with the peasants and slumdwellers thirty years ago, we have to develop with our learners our own methods, our own techniques, our own activities, our own curriculum, in our own reality.

Part 2

WHAT POPULAR EDUCATION IS... AND ISN'T

To understand the Paulo Freire methodology,
it is necessary to analyze what is meant by
methodology, and how it offers a framework
for the use of educational techniques...

Many educators in the United States confuse methodology with educational techniques, and think that practicing popular education is as simple as using group discussion, role-playing, group research, videos, slides, and other techniques used by popular educators.

These techniques can be used for all kinds of objectives that are the opposite of popular education goals—for example, to push workers in a factory to produce more, so the companies can have more profits.

Educational techniques are tools we use following the principles of the methodology.

Even when these techniques are used on curricula developed about real problems of the learners, this is not popular education, if the *methodology*—in particular, the three step process: TO SEE, TO JUDGE, TO ACT—is not used.

EXAMPLES OF EDUCATIONAL TECHNIQUES USED IN POPULAR EDUCATION:

- **Forming small subgroups for discussion, followed by general discussion in a plenary**

- **The use of illustrated charts, cartoons, comic book stories**

- **The use of videos, slides, films**

- **Participative activities like mock trials, role-playing, discussion continuum, group research**

- **The use of puppet theater**

- **Graphics made in and for the class, such as "problem maps," "problem trees," "strategic maps," etc.**

The basics of the methodology are outlined in the chart on the next page. First the educators have to learn what are the main problems the learners are experiencing in their workplace, community, or organization. We call these problems the *generative themes.* They have to talk with the people in their communities, to live with them, when this is possible, to understand their lives, their way of thinking, their culture.

Having identified the generative themes, the next step is to produce the codes. A code is a material representation of the generative theme. A code can be a drawing, a video, a photo, a puppet skit, a tape with an interview, a report, a role play, etc.

The best way to produce the codes about the principal problems in the lives of the learners is by working *with* the learners.

THE THREE-STEP INDUCTIVE QUESTIONING PROCESS

The *code* (a problem map for example) is the starting point of an inductive questioning process that has three steps:

First step: TO SEE the situation lived by the participants. This moment can be subdivided into three steps, when the participants have no experience in participation in any kind of grassroots organizations. They can be shy, afraid of talking about their problems, so to make it easier for them, break it down . . .

... Step 1: TO SEE

1) Ask the participants to describe the situation presented in the code. Write their description on the blackboard.

2) Ask them to define the principal problems presented in this situation, and write this on the blackboard.

3) Ask them if they ever had similar problems, or if they know somebody who had similar problems.

Second step: **TO JUDGE** the situation. The educator asks questions and coordinates activities that help the class form their analysis of the immediate causes and root causes of the problems. This analysis can be represented in a "problem tree," illustrating the participants own descriptions of their problems, including causes and consequences.

To be able to analyze the socioeconomic, political, and cultural causes of their problems, the participants must know how to use sociological analytical tools. They must have a basic knowledge of the structures of the society they live in, of the workings of this society, the class divisions, etc. It is the role

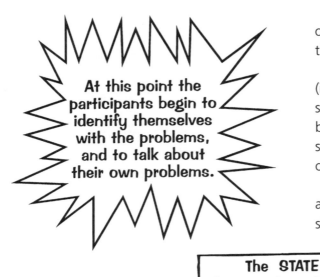

At this point the participants begin to identify themselves with the problems, and to talk about their own problems.

of the educator to provide the learners with these analytical tools.

In Brazil, educators developed a *cartilha* (illustrated pamphlet) entitled "How does society work?" (A page from it appears below.) They found this an effective resource for study and discussion by all kinds of students.

Third step: **TO ACT** to change this situation. To be able to really change the situation lived by the participants, they

The STATE
The state is the combination of people and institutions that holds and exercises power—society's management

The LAWS that govern society

The MILITARY and The POLICE

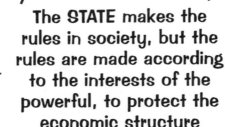

The STATE makes the rules in society, but the rules are made according to the interests of the powerful, to protect the economic structure

The BUREAUCRACY of agencies and departments

The JUDICIAL system

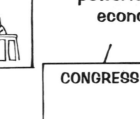

CONGRESS

The EXECUTIVE branch of the government (president, cabinet, and armed forces)

have to plan their short term actions and long term actions. It's not possible for a community group or a workers' group to change the society they live in by themselves alone. Real social change requires a long term plan, engaging many groups, organizations, communities. But it is possible to plan and accomplish short term actions that are part of a long term plan. To help plan this action, organize practical discussion into a "strategic map." One mistake often made by educators in the United States is to discuss and plan short term actions without a long term plan to really change the situation of the participants in society, let alone a plan to change the whole society. Without a long-term plan, or at least an attempt to draft one, these actions end up reconciling the participants to the very situation—and the socioeconomic, political, and cultural system behind it—that created the problems in the first place. On the following pages are examples from a group of neighborhood residents and a group of health care workers in New York City.

Making "problem maps" helps to focus the class on
the learners' own problems as they identify them.

This problem map of a New York City neighborhood was produced by LOCAL RESIDENTS as a class assignment.

A group of HEALTH CARE WORKERS
and activists compared notes on the
problems they have to deal with.

This problem map was the collective result.

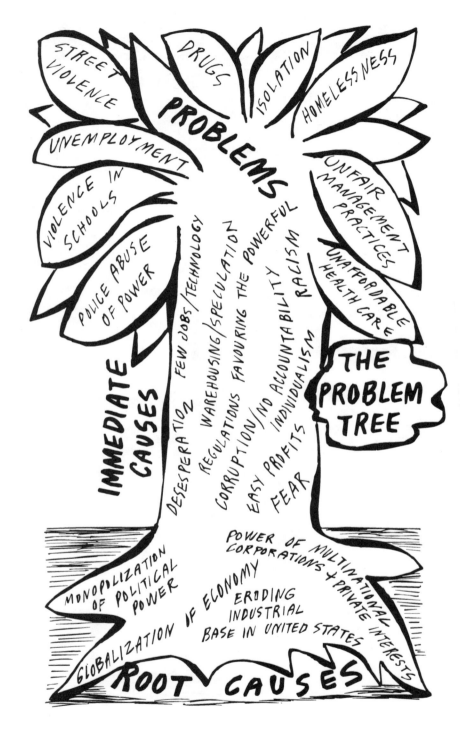

This problem tree was made by the same group of **NEIGHBORHOOD RESIDENTS** who did the drawing of the problem map on pages 32-33.

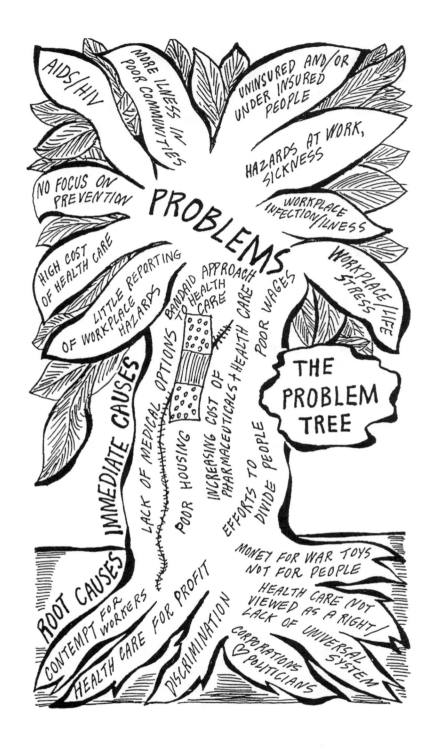

The **HEALTH CARE WORKERS** mentioned on page 34 drew their own problem tree after discussing their principle problems.

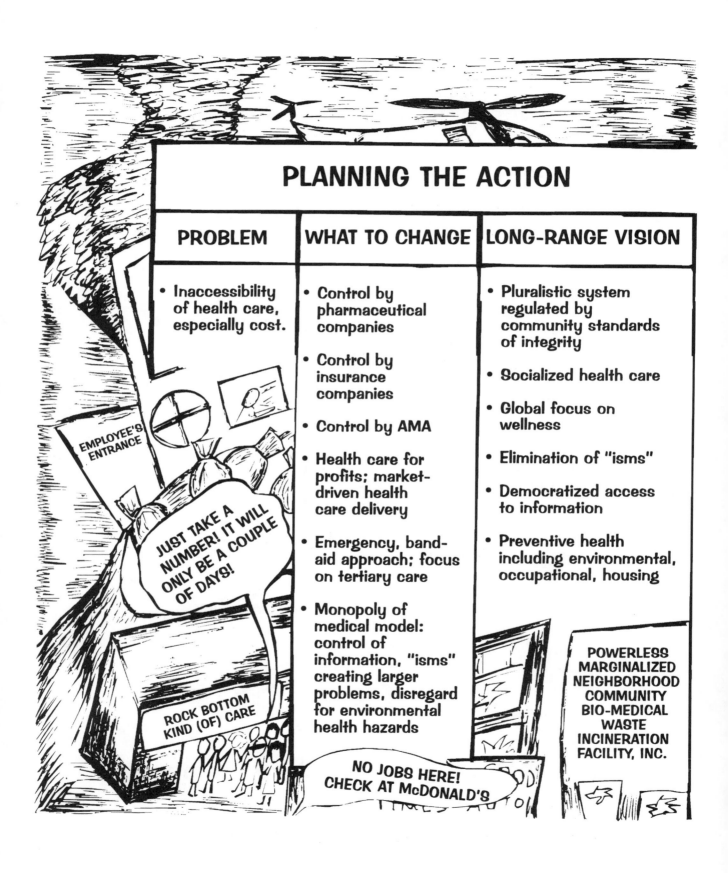

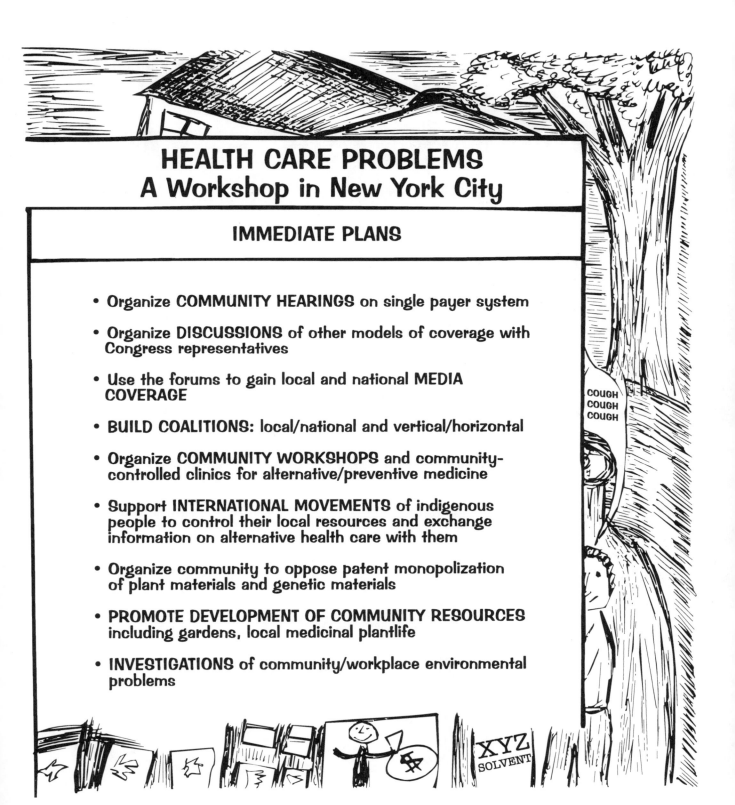

HEALTH CARE PROBLEMS
A Workshop in New York City

IMMEDIATE PLANS

- Organize COMMUNITY HEARINGS on single payer system

- Organize DISCUSSIONS of other models of coverage with Congress representatives

- Use the forums to gain local and national MEDIA COVERAGE

- BUILD COALITIONS: local/national and vertical/horizontal

- Organize COMMUNITY WORKSHOPS and community-controlled clinics for alternative/preventive medicine

- Support INTERNATIONAL MOVEMENTS of indigenous people to control their local resources and exchange information on alternative health care with them

- Organize community to oppose patent monopolization of plant materials and genetic materials

- PROMOTE DEVELOPMENT OF COMMUNITY RESOURCES including gardens, local medicinal plantlife

- INVESTIGATIONS of community/workplace environmental problems

COUGH
COUGH
COUGH

XYZ
SOLVENT

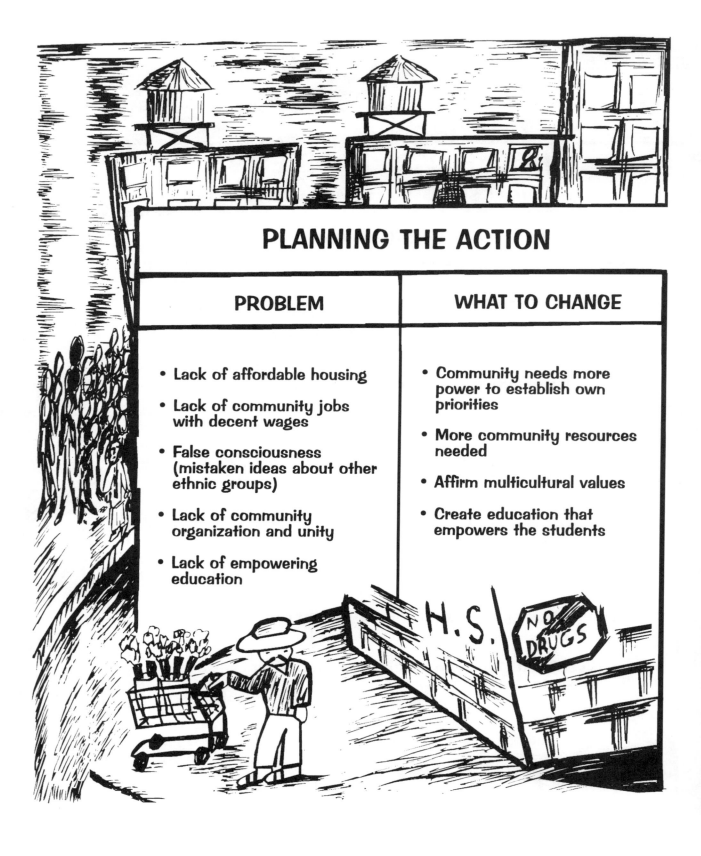

PLANNING THE ACTION

PROBLEM	WHAT TO CHANGE
• Lack of affordable housing	• Community needs more power to establish own priorities
• Lack of community jobs with decent wages	• More community resources needed
• False consciousness (mistaken ideas about other ethnic groups)	• Affirm multicultural values
• Lack of community organization and unity	• Create education that empowers the students
• Lack of empowering education	

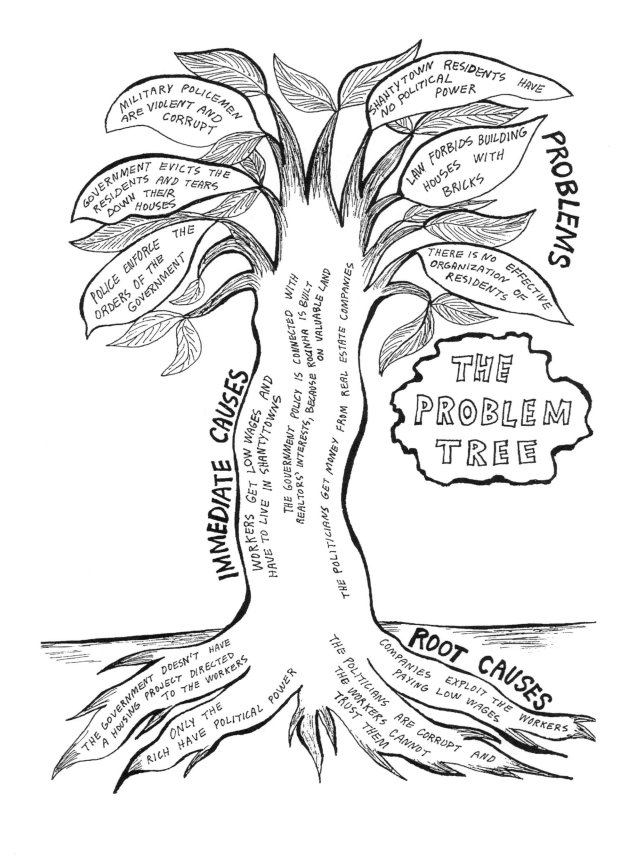

This problem tree and the strategic map that follows were created by residents of Rocinha, a Rio de Janeiro shantytown (population 200,000). The followup to the Rocinha residents' planning took the form of action that developed into a struggle that lasted seven years. In the end, the objective of the short term plan was accomplished:

- the residents built their homes with bricks;
- the government changed the policy of destroying the shantytowns and evicting residents;
- possession of the land by the residents became an accepted fact and began to be legalized.

The struggle didn't stop there. They went after other problems like police violence and drug gangs.

PLANNING THE ACTION

PROBLEM

- Law forbids building houses with bricks

- Police enforce government orders

- Law is connected with realtors' interests, because Rocinha is built on valuable land

- No effective residents organization; the neighborhood association has been useless since 1968

WHAT TO CHANGE

- The laws

- The power relationship between residents of Rocinha and the government (police, local and national executive branch, legislature)

SHANTYTOWN OF ROCINHA
Rio de Janeiro

LONG-RANGE VISION	IMMEDIATE PLANS
• To create an urban policy controlled by the community organizations • To create mechanisms of collective power in Rio • To change the socioeconomic, political, and cultural structures of Brazil	• To organize the residents around each struggle dealing with housing construction • To use the neighborhood association as the organizing instrument of the residents • To create a house-building committee in the association • To elect directors for the committee • To publicly denounce police violence and lawbreaking • To lobby state congress representatives to support new laws and a new shantytown policy

ACTIVITIES FOR THE EDUCATORS

Form a popular education class *about* popular education. The participants are divided into subgroups of five to six. Each subgroup has a facilitator, who coordinates the discussion.

Each subgroup answers three questions:

1) What is the principal goal of popular education? Is it political or not? Why?

2) Define popular education.

3) How can you use popular education in your workplace/ community/organizing activities?

After meeting for twenty or thirty minutes, the subgroups gather in a plenary. Each subgroup selects someone to write a summary of the answers and reads this to the plenary, and the facilitator writes these answers on a blackboard or sheets of paper. The partici- pants are free to intervene, giving more explanations about their answers. The facilitator then coordinates a general discussion about the answers, taking care that all aspects of the problems are discussed.

Turn to page 124 for "The Basics" of popular education in practice.

Part 3

A Curriculum for Making Sense of the Media

The objective of this handbook is to develop a popular education curriculum through which learners can develop a critical analysis of the mass media and the alternative media.

In today's world, the most important mechanism used by the capitalist system to dominate the people is the *ideology* transmitted through the mass media. Examples of this ideology include the idea that "the United States is an equal opportunity society," or that "everyone who works hard, is honest, and stays inside the system can become rich or be president."

The objective of this curriculum is to enable learners to use analytical tools to understand the ideology transmitted through commercial advertising, political campaigns, electronic and print news reportage, soap operas, sitcoms, educational TV programs, etc.

In the process, the learners produce their own alternative media, including puppets, graphic materials, comic book stories, illustrated charts, newsletters and videos. These forms of popular communication are examined in more detail in Part 4.

The curriculum is geared for use by high school teachers, college teachers (mainly social sciences and communications teachers), community center educators, and organizers of all kinds.

We assume a class size of at least ten learners, who regularly break into subgroups of five or six for discussions and activities.

Materials needed will include a blackboard; video recorder, camera and tapes; recent magazines and newspapers; and art supplies. It's always good to have a still camera on hand to record the experience.

1. GET ACQUAINTED

When beginning any workshop, course, or class of popular education, the first thing to do is learn about the participants.

We can use various techniques. The participants can be divided into couples (if possible, persons who are not acquainted), and each person interviews the other for six minutes, asking their name, background, profession, workplace, and expectations about the course. Each one of them then speaks aloud, introducing the person interviewed.

Or: Each person draws their life journey as a map. After this, each person shows their map to the class and explains it.

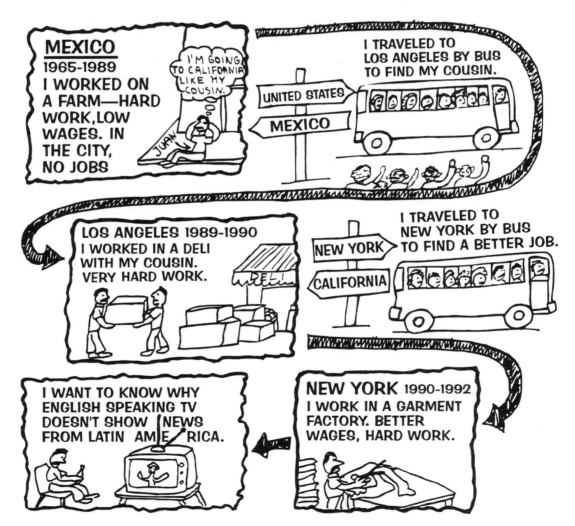

2. FOCUSING THE GROUP: THE CODE

To bring the participants together around the study/discussion topic, and to "break the ice" (cut through problems like fatalism and unfamiliarity with the process), the class produces a *code*. As described in Part 2, the code is a visual representation of the situation under discussion as experienced and commonly seen by the participants.

The best way to produce the code is to ask the participants to produce a puppet show or skit about the consumer society in which the principal character is a compulsive buyer who believes in commercial advertising. Other characters can include: a friend who is critical of consumer society, the salesperson in a shop, etc.

Form subgroups of five or six people; each subgroup produces a skit that is presented to the whole audience.

Give the subgroups thirty minutes to develop a five-to-ten-minute skit, or produce a cartoon or comic book story about the same theme. (See below.)

Alternatively, you can produce the code with a group of educators and present it to the class: perform a skit, display a drawing, etc., to represent the generative theme of consumerism.

3. THE INDUCTIVE QUESTIONING PROCESS

Ask the participants questions about the presentation of the code, such as:

1) **Why does the compulsive buyer believe that to buy things is to acquire happiness?**

2) **Do you think that this idea that "buying is happiness" is believed by most people in the United States? Why?**

3) Do you think that to buy things is the most important thing in life? What do you think are more important things in life?

The objective of this activity is to question the values and the ideology of the consumerist society.

For discussions, each subgroup needs to call on a member with some experience in leading group dialogue to act as *facilitator*, and a *relater* who writes down the participants' answers. Have each subgroup take twenty to thirty minutes for the discussion. All the participants then get together in plenary and the relaters read the answers of each subgroup; each person is free to explain more about the answers of his/her subgroup, if they think it is necessary.

Write the answers on the blackboard and coordinate a general discussion about them, making a synthesis of the final result of the talk.

Next, focus on magazine advertisements. Each subgroup analyzes three or four magazine ads for thirty minutes. Choose the ads according to the characteristics of the participants. Each subgroup answers these questions:

- What do you see?
- What is the objective of this ad?
- What people would buy these goods?
- Would you buy these goods because of this ad?
- Why?

4. DEMYSTIFYING THE TECHNOLOGY OF PERSUASION

The facilitator explains how an ad is produced, using charts.

The discussion is in three parts:

1) **Who is the target audience for the ad?**

   To study the characteristics of the target audience, the group of people they want to sell goods and services to, the advertising professionals use all kinds of market research techniques—surveys, focus groups. Through these techniques they understand the way a group thinks, their desires and expectations, their way of living, etc. Based on this data, the professionals develop advertising campaigns.

2) **What is the objective of the advertising campaign?**

   The principal objective is always to sell goods and services. But a campaign can also seek to create the market for a new product.

3) **What are the methods used to convince people to buy the goods and services?**

The advertising professionals use many different methods for convincing people. This is an actual technology, the technology of persuasion.

For example, in the 1950's in Brazil, multinational companies wanted to create a new market for deodorants. The people of Brazil

HOW TO PRODUCE AN AD

THE TECHNOLOGY OF PERSUASION

1. WHO IS THE TARGET AUDIENCE?

Describe their class, culture, way of life; their problems, desires, dreams expectations. Use surveys, focus groups, polls, statistics, etc.

2. WHAT IS THE OBJECTIVE OF THE AD YOU WANT TO PRODUCE?

- To sell a product
- To create a product for a new market
- To replace an old product with new one

3. WHAT METHOD SHOULD BE USED TO OBTAIN THIS OBJECTIVE?

What are the best arguments to use with the target audience according to their culture, their way of thinking, their desires and dreams?

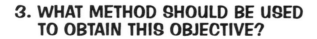

didn't use deodorants—they used talcum powder made of fine cornstarch and baking soda that was very effective and had no harmful side-effects. Brazilians also take one or more baths a day, since it's a tropical country.

The companies produced national advertising campaigns for television, radio, and magazines, showing people who smelled bad, were very unpopular, lost their boy/girl friends, lost good jobs, etc., because they didn't use deodorants.

In a few months, there was a new market in Brazil for deodorants because most people were convinced through the advertising campaign of the need to use deodorants.

Advertising campaigns are also used to change an old product for a new one.

Here are some of the most common methods used in commercial advertising:

MARKETING METHODS
THE TECHNOLOGY OF PERSUASION

1. Celebrity endorsement

2. Appeal to social status

3. Appeal to competitive instinct

4. Appeal to sexuality

5. Appeal to "manhood values"

6. Appeal to "family values"

7. Showing the superiority of the product

8. Appeal to feelings of insecurity

9. Appeal to bargaining instinct

10. Appeal to the "exotic," the different

11. Shock appeal: special effects

12. Appeal to ecological values (natural products)

13. Appeal to the pursuit of fun and games

14. Appeal to peer values

15. Making fun of advertising (so people feel they are not being deceived)

16. Appeal to the wish for youth and beauty

CELEBRITY ENDORSEMENT

One of the most-used marketing methods. A movie star, sports star, or other big name praises the product, saying that she/he uses it because of its superior quality.

APPEAL TO "MANHOOD VALUES"

The product is identified with "manly" images: cowboys, athletes, strong adventurous men in scenes of action.

SINGING THE PRAISES

The product is to be praised for its alleged qualities and is compared favorably to so-called inferior rival brands.

This explanation by the facilitator cannot last for more than fifteen minutes. Then s/he answers questions from the subgroup. The facilitator also asks participants to give examples of ads that use the methods already explained.

5. ANALYSIS OF MAGAZINE AND TV ADS

Explain that the participants are going to analyze ads, answering the questions posed earlier:

1) **What is the target audience?**

2) **What is the objective of this ad?**

3) **What was the method used to attain this objective?**

The subgroups analyze three or four magazine ads for twenty minutes. After that, the relaters tell the whole class the results of the subgroup analysis, showing the ads. The participants are encouraged to ask questions and give suggestions, analyzing other aspects of the ads.

Show a video with a selection of TV ads, preferably the most familiar and representative of various advertising techniques. After each ad, the class analyzes it, answering the three questions. One person writes the answers on the blackboard while the educator coordinates the questioning process.

6. EXPLAINING THE REASONS FOR COMMERCIAL ADVERTISING

Initiate a discussion on the creation and development of commercial advertising, the technology of persuasion, using the chart on the next page.

In the market economy, there is competition between companies to sell the goods and services they produce. The companies have to convince consumers to buy their goods and services; they use a highly developed technology of persuasion in commercial advertising.

The goal of the companies is to get the maximum profit, so they plan their production according to this goal, not according to the real needs of the consumers. They produce things that are useless or harmful, like cigarettes, toxic pesticides, dangerous drugs, guns and armaments, etc.

The principal ideological mechanism to support this economic system is commercial advertising through the mass media.

One long-range alternative would be an economic system with general production policies, controlled by the public. The companies would produce goods and services reflecting the real needs of the people, and not only for getting maximum profit. In this society, there would be no need to use the technology of persuasion to convince consumers to buy goods and services. Commercial advertising would be used to explain the qualities of the goods and services, rather than to manipulate emotions.

This explanation should take fifteen minutes. Answer the questions of the participants and ask them to give examples of

useless and harmful products produced in this society. Then the subgroups reassemble to answer the questions:

1) Do you think that this economic system, based on consumerism and advertising, is good for the people? Why? Do you think there is a real need for so many different brands and kinds of products?

2) The majority of people in the world suffer from hunger and don't have the basic necessities to live with dignity, and the minority live in an extravagant consumer society. How is this situation rationalized? What do you think?

3) What do you think should be done to change the consumer society?

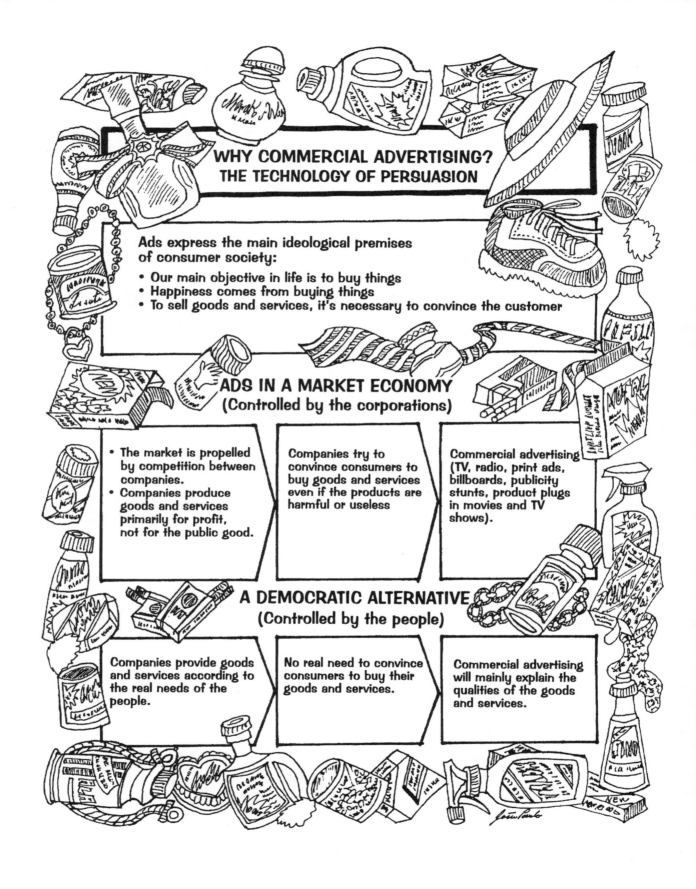

WHY COMMERCIAL ADVERTISING?
THE TECHNOLOGY OF PERSUASION

Ads express the main ideological premises
of consumer society:

- Our main objective in life is to buy things
- Happiness comes from buying things
- To sell goods and services, it's necessary to convince the customer

ADS IN A MARKET ECONOMY
(Controlled by the corporations)

- The market is propelled by competition between companies.
- Companies produce goods and services primarily for profit, not for the public good.

Companies try to convince consumers to buy goods and services even if the products are harmful or useless

Commercial advertising (TV, radio, print ads, billboards, publicity stunts, product plugs in movies and TV shows).

A DEMOCRATIC ALTERNATIVE
(Controlled by the people)

Companies provide goods and services according to the real needs of the people.

No real need to convince consumers to buy their goods and services.

Commercial advertising will mainly explain the qualities of the goods and services.

After the subgroup discussions, as the relaters tell the results to the plenary, write the summary of the answers on the board. The participants are encouraged to give suggestions and to criticize the answers of the subgroups.

The objective of this activity is to develop the critical consciousness of the participants in relation to the consumer society and the market economy controlled by the corporations.

7. THE GAME OF THE TRUTHFUL ADS

Each subgroup creates their own commercial ads using collages, photos, drawings, cartoons, etc. Playing off "real ads" (cigarettes, cars, beauty products, etc.), the participants turn the tables by telling the truth about the goods, as previously discussed.

Each subgroup acts out their own "TV ads," also inspired by real ads. This exercise is more difficult, because they need some props to make good ads. One way to do this is to ask the subgroups to choose the ad they want to produce, and bring the props they need to the next class, when they produce it.

Ask subgroups: What can you do about commercial advertising? Discuss strategies to demystify commercial advertising, and some practical action. The relaters bring the answers of the subgroups to the plenary, followed by a final discussion using the chart "Planning the Action" (see Part 2).

If necessary for clarification, replay the video.

The relaters present the answers of the subgroups at the plenary, and there is a general discussion.

8. ANALYZING THE NEWS: TV

Show a video of part of the newscast of the day before. The subgroups analyze the news, answering the questions:

1) **What did you see? What were the main issues presented in the news?**

2) **Do you think that the news reports presented were factual? Are there other aspects of the story they didn't present? Is there some bias on the presentation of the story?**

3) **Why did they choose these issues and not others? Can you name other more important issues that should be on the news and were not? Why were they not presented?**

9. ANALYZING THE NEWS: PRINT

Show newspaper and magazine reports with different versions of the same story, and ask the subgroups to analyze them, answering the questions:

1) **What are the differences presented in these versions of the same fact?**

2) **What are the objectives of the authors in presenting these different versions?**

3) **What were the methods used by the authors to make the public think what they wanted them to think?**

After the subgroup discussion, the relaters present the results in the plenary, followed by a general discussion.

10. Control of the Mass Media and the Role of Ideology

Explain the ownership and functioning of the mass media companies, using the chart on the next page.

Explain the concept of ideology, using the chart on the following page:

During the explanation, give examples of ideology transmitted through popular TV programs, the commercial ads and news they have already analyzed; for example, by constantly invoking the need to be a "winner" and not a "loser"—the ideology of the competitive society—children are trained to compete with their peers, to always win by whatever means, and to feel frustrated when they lose. *Individualism* is the value

MASS MEDIA COMPANIES
TV, RADIO, NEWSPAPERS, MAGAZINES

- The objective of the mass media companies is to get the maximum profits.
- The profits come from the sale of commercial advertising.
- The policies of mass media companies are controlled by the corporations that buy ads.
- The mass media act as an instrument for transmitting the dominant ideology in society—an ideology built around the concerns and interests of the classes that have power. The objective of this ideology is the acceptance of the systems by everyone in society.

USES OF MASS MEDIA

- To sell goods and services
- To entertain
- To inform
- To educate

] IDEOLOGY is transmitted through all these activities

The IDEOLOGY of our society is the set of ideas—the way of thinking—that surrounds us all our lives, and that we perceive as our own ideas. These ideas are introduced through mechanisms controlled by society's ruling classes.

The objective of IDEOLOGY is to make people accept society as it is.

transmitted—not *cooperation* with others for the benefit of the community. This explanation should take fifteen minutes.

After the explanation, the subgroups discuss the following questions:

1) Is the principal goal of the mass media companies to inform, entertain, and educate the public?

2) Do you think you can believe the information transmitted through the mass media (TV, radio, newspapers, magazines)? Why?

3) What is the role of public television, public radio and independent newspapers supposed to be in our society? Do you think this role is being accomplished? Why?

4) What do you think should be done to democratize the mass media, to bring the mass media nearer to the interests of the public, and away from the interests of the corporations?

After the subgroup discussion, the relater brings the answers to the general assembly and a general discussion follows. Write a summary of the results on the blackboard.

Ask the participants to give examples of ideology transmitted through the mass media and coordinate a general discussion on the content of radio, TV and print news reportage.

Follow this discussion by asking the subgroups to analyze newspaper news, magazine news, and TV news. Refer to news stories chosen for their social and political relevance, answering the questions:

1) What is the objective of this report/article, and what do the authors want us to think?

2) What methods did they use to attain this objective?

Again, the relaters bring the answers to the plenary for a general discussion.

11. THE GAME OF THE TRUTHFUL NEWS

The subgroups produce newspapers/magazine reports about important issues, related to their lives, to their experiences, that have been the subject of news in the mass media. The goal is to expose and demystify the ideological bias of mass media reports on these issues.

To produce these reports in newspaper/magazine format, make and use collages of headlines, drawings, or photos. These reports can be made in a simple form—the important thing is the content. If this is not possible, use the participants' own real life knowledge about these issues, and invent interviews with imaginary people drawn from their experience.

The subgroups can also produce TV news, using interviews with members of the subgroup. If possible, they can make videos with real interviews in the community, etc.

The subgroups present their productions to the plenary for a general discussion, with the whole group analyzing the differences between their reports and the reports of the mass media.

12. ANALYZING POLITICAL ADVERTISING

Present a typical campaign ad from a recent election. Have subgroups discuss:

1) Who is the target audience of this ad?

2) What is the objective of this ad?

3) What is the method used to convince people? Would you be convinced by this ad? Why?

The relaters take the answers to the plenary for a general discussion.

13. ANALYZING POPULAR TV PROGRAMS

The participants analyze a popular program they like to watch (soap opera, sitcom, talk shows, etc.). To help them, a video with segments of the program is used. Ask questions that provoke analysis of the ideology transmitted through this program; for example, character portrayals that show any kind of bias, the political implications of characters' actions, etc.

This curriculum can be used with groups of varying backgrounds, from early teens to seniors. The educator has only to adapt the language and the themes to each group. It has been used with middle-class teenagers, workers, labor leaders, teachers, and inner-city youngsters, in each case successfully.

When participants learn how to understand and use the analytical tools to demystify the mass media, they are vaccinated against the ideology transmitted through them. When they see an ad, a TV news program, a sitcom, they are able to analyze the real objectives of all these productions, and are not manipulated by them. This process of ideological liberation is essential for any kind of effective action to change the unjust structures of society.

CLIMBING THE LADDER

THE IDEOLOGY OF THE EQUAL OPPORTUNITY SOCIETY: One who works hard and is honest and talented can become a millionaire or the President of the United States.

The reality: Opportunities are far from equal. The upper class minority of the population has good opportunities for education, jobs, etc. The middle class has some opportunities, though not as many. And the working class has few opportunities; only the very lucky and very talented few can climb the ladder.

DIRTY HARRY

THE IDEOLOGY OF THE GOOD GUYS VS. THE BAD GUYS: The good guys are the defenders of the system, the bad guys attack the system. The good guys always win, even though they often have to use violence to defeat the bad guys.

The reality: The guys who attack the system are not always bad, and guys who defend the system can be bad. The system is not always good, and needs many changes just to keep its own promises.

LITTLE ORPHAN ANNIE

THE IDEOLOGY OF INDIVIDUALISTIC ACTION: Problems in society are caused by the individual actions of the bad guys and not by the existing socio-economic, political, and cultural structures; consequently, these problems can be resolved through individual actions within the same structures.

The reality: The problem is not that business owners and politicians are wicked and greedy, but that the system in which they live and which determines their activities was not constructed to benefit the majority of the people.

Part 4

Popular Communication

Puppet theater characters: the union organizer Veronica Johnson and Altagracia.

In popular education methodology, an important part is played by popular communication—the techniques for communicating with the participants in the learning process. In Latin America, popular educators use puppet/human theater, audiovisuals, radio programs, comic book stories, illustrated charts and posters, flyers, newsletters, etc.

These educational materials are produced by educators and members of the community and/or organizations engaged in the learning process. Graphic materials are invariably used in the courses, and as a means to inform, organize, and mobilize the communities.

This section will explain how to produce puppet theater and graphic materials in popular education, based on the experience of more than fifteen years working with popular organizations in Brazil.

THE USE OF PUPPET THEATER

All over the world, educators who use the Paulo Freire methodology have developed new techniques suitable to the reality lived by the learners. One of the most efficient tools to be used in the classrooms is the puppet theater. In the USA, puppet theater

The boss and former President Bush.

Altagracia.

is mostly used for children, but puppet theater for adults is a very old tradition in every continent for cultural and educational purposes. It is used in health campaigns (about AIDS and other epidemics, drugs, nutrition, sanitary instruction, etc.); union activities (organizing, union elections, strikes, etc.); community organizing, religious instruction, and schools for child and adult education.

Puppet theater can be extremely effective for educational purposes when people use puppets for discussing issues that they would not feel comfortable discussing with other people. For example, there is a cultural taboo about sex education in most countries in Africa. But puppets can talk about sex without shocking anybody, so puppet theater is used in AIDS prevention campaigns.

This phenomenon of feeling free to hear and to talk with puppets about their most important problems is recognized by educators internationally.

In popular education, educators and learners create stories with the puppets about generative themes, and these stories are developed into learning activities of all kinds: literacy lessons, language lessons, geography, history, economics, political science, health instruction, labor law, immigration law, etc.

By this method, the learners take an active part in the learning process, are much more interested, and don't forget what they learn.

Each educator has to learn through practice the best way to use this pedagogic tool with the learners. Once again, the activities, lessons, exercises, etc., follow the three steps: TO SEE, TO JUDGE, TO ACT. With enough experience, the educator can create new activities with each new group of learners, from all kinds of cultures and backgrounds.

Puppets can be used as a code for presenting generative themes in any number of educational and organizing settings.

The use of puppets acquires greater importance in this society as a counter to the dominating ideology transmitted by the mass media. Puppets can be used as an alternative media, to stimulate analysis of society and to help find the ways to change it.

A PUPPET WORKSHOP: ALTAGRACIA COMES TO AMERICA

In 1991 we conducted a puppet workshop for the Consortium for Worker Education, an organization of twenty-seven trade unions in New York City. In this workshop, the participants chose generative themes from their real life problems, the problems of Latin American workers in the garment industry in New York. The themes were: undocumented workers, cultural conflicts, exploitation, and sexual harassment in the workplace, union organizing, and U.S. government economic policy. The objective is to make the audience participate in the story, discuss the problems, and present solutions.

The participants invented the characters of the puppets they made.

- **ALTAGRACIA**—a Dominican woman who came to New York to her cousin's home, to find a job. In the Dominican Republic there were no good jobs for her.

- **ASUNCIÓN**—Altagracia's cousin, who has lived in New York for seven years and works in a garment factory.

- **RAFAEL, aka RALPH**—Asunción's husband, who changed his name because he wants to be an American. He doesn't work. He wants to be a pop star with the band "New Cubans on the Block."

Big Joe and his pet rat.

- **Grandmother DOLORES**—Asunción's mother. She hates life in the USA, refuses to learn English, and wants to go back to Santo Domingo.

- **BIG JOE**—the foreman of the garment factory where Asunción works. He's a bad man who sexually harasses the workers.

- **MARIA**—Another worker in the factory, Asunción's friend.

- **LINMIN**—a Chinese worker in the factory. She is afraid of being dismissed if they try to unionize the shop. She is also afraid of union activities, because she knows about another factory that was closed and transferred to Mexico when workers tried to organize.

- **VERONICA JOHNSON**—the union organizer, born in Jamaica. She is invited by Asunción to go to a meeting in her house, to talk about the union and how to organize the workers.

Asunción and Altagracia in the demonstration for union elections.

Speaker of the House Newt Gingrich and the monster of the budget cuts.

- The BOSS—the factory's owner. He is furious when he discovers the union organizing activities of the workers. He asks for President Bush's help, because he is a Republican.

- PRESIDENT BUSH—he shows up when the workers are demanding an election to unionize the factory, and discusses with them the situation of workers in the country.

At the same time that the participants made the hand puppets, they talked about their characters and developed the outline of the story, called "Altagracia Comes to America." When the puppets were ready, the participants began rehearsing with them and developed the story dialogue—not learned by heart, but always improvised. The story changed all the time, as the puppets discussed with the audience the problems they were living, asking their advice, sometimes contradicting them, sometimes accepting their opinion.

The story "Altagracia Comes to America" was presented in a workshop at the Paulo Freire conference held at the New School for Social Research in December 1991. In the last scene, the workers and the union organizer discuss with President Bush the situation of the working class. Bush defends the system, saying that America is the paradise of the free market economy and the market resolves all problems by itself. The workers deny this, saying that the market economy didn't resolve such very serious problems as health care, unemployment, low wages, housing, education, drugs, crime, etc. Bush says that they chose this system when they voted for him. The workers answer that they didn't vote for him, and that 1992 is coming, and President Bush will see what happens in the election—he is going to be thrown out!

President Bush flees, saying that he has an urgent appointment, and the workers finish the story singing a labor song in Spanish.

The real President Bush, at this time, was high in the polls, and all the political analysts believed that he was invincible. But the puppets were right in their analysis, and turned out to be the best political analysts in the USA! Their analysis was made from the point of view of the workers, and so was closer to the socioeconomic reality lived by millions in this country.

The puppet story was used as a code in ESL and GED classes in the Consortium for Worker Education. The results are described in the concluding part of this book.

HOW TO DO A PUPPET SHOW

In using puppets as a popular education vehicle, it's useful to start involving the participants at the actual creation of the puppets. The characters should reflect the lived experience of the participants, as interpreted by the participants themselves.

In this section, the process of doing a puppet show is broken down step by step: making the puppets, making the stage, making scenery, developing the stories.

The first step in this process is discussion among the participants to choose the generative theme; the characters follow from that. The participants discuss the themes most suitable for developing into a story.

To develop a theme into a story, the participants need to answer three questions:

Public school students in the puppet workshop at the Community Arts Center (CAMBA) in Brooklyn, New York.

- **What are the basic shared problems in the participants' lives?**

- **What are the real, socioeconomic causes of this problem?**

- **What can the participants do to resolve this problem?**

At this point a story outline is drafted, featuring the puppet characters. The dialogue comes later.

In the story, these questions are to be answered by the puppets and by the audience, through the dialogue and their interaction.

MAKING THE PUPPETS

The participants draw what the puppets each one will make will look like, deciding on and incorporating the main characteristics. Use photos, cartoons, drawings as models for your puppets.

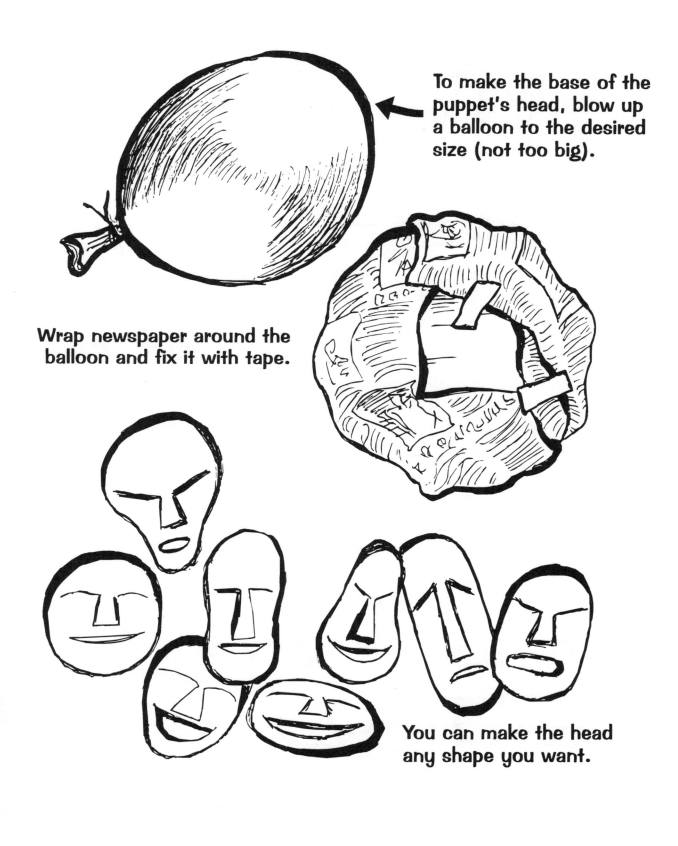

To make the base of the puppet's head, blow up a balloon to the desired size (not too big).

Wrap newspaper around the balloon and fix it with tape.

You can make the head any shape you want.

The heads are formed and given faces with newspaper strips soaked in wheat flour paste, paper towels, and aluminum foil.

Mix the wheat flour with water, put over heat and stir until it boils.

GLUE

Soak newspaper strips in paste and apply to the head in layers to make the features.

Pay attention to where you want to put the nose, eyes, mouth, ears.

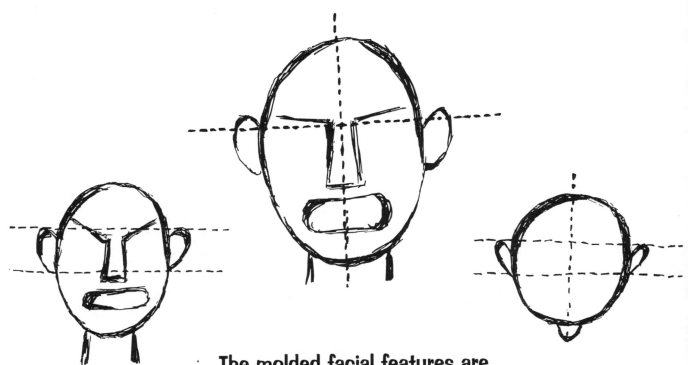

The molded facial features are shaded. Make sure the molded features are symmetrical.

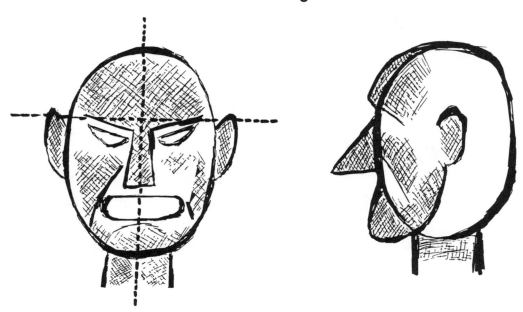

Use aluminum foil to make the base for the molded features—shape the foil and tape it to the head.

For the ears to project from the head, make a tab from the shaped foil and tape to head.

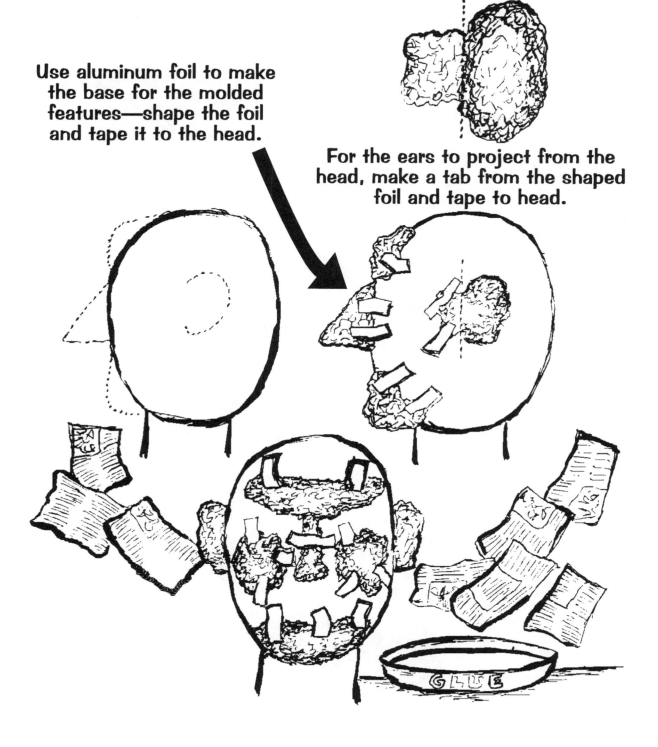

GLUE

Apply paste-soaked
newspaper strips
over molded foil.

Glue the tube inside the
puppet's neck-hole and
paste newspaper strips
around it until you have
the proper thickness.

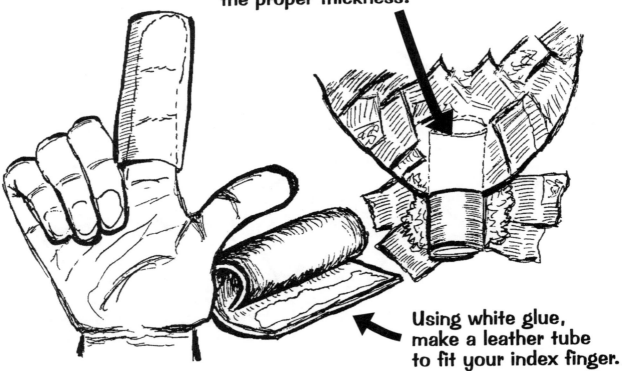

Using white glue,
make a leather tube
to fit your index finger.

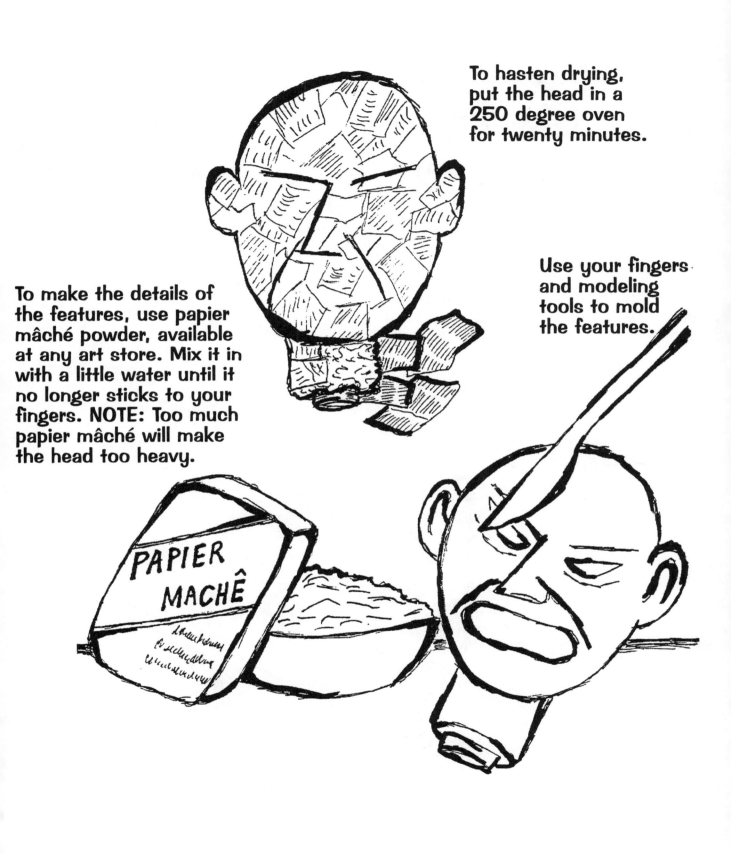

To hasten drying,
put the head in a
250 degree oven
for twenty minutes.

To make the details of
the features, use papier
mâché powder, available
at any art store. Mix it in
with a little water until it
no longer sticks to your
fingers. NOTE: Too much
papier mâché will make
the head too heavy.

Use your fingers
and modeling
tools to mold
the features.

PAPIER
MACHÊ

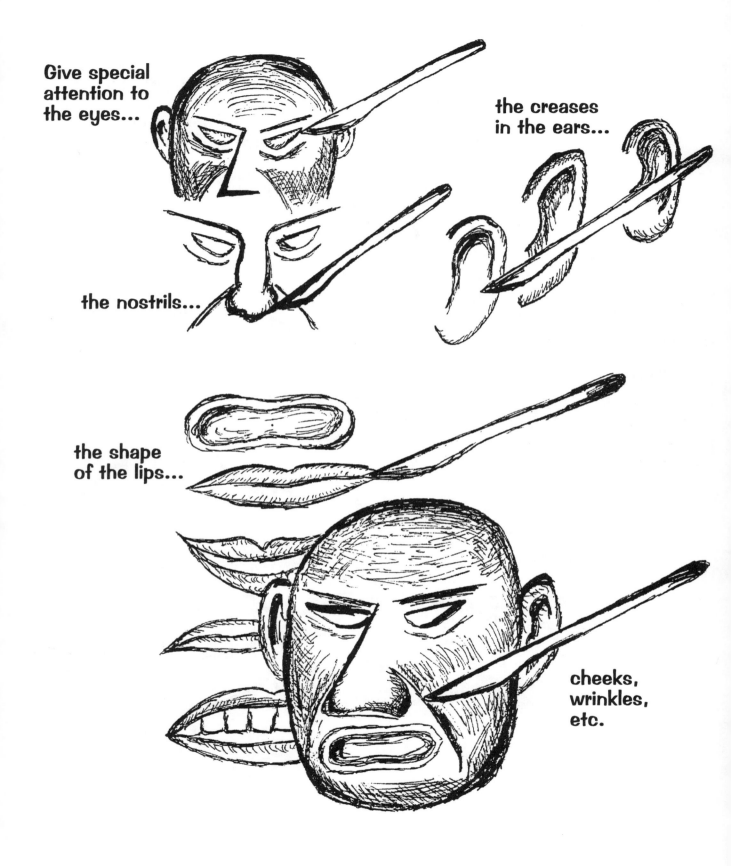

Give special attention to the eyes...

the creases in the ears...

the nostrils...

the shape of the lips...

cheeks, wrinkles, etc.

When the papier mâché is dry, use cutting tools to put the finishing touches on the face.

Then cover the head with a thin layer of gesso or spackle, using fingers or a brush for application.

SANDPAPER

When the gesso is dry, sandpaper the head until its surface is smooth.

GESSO

SPACKLING PASTE

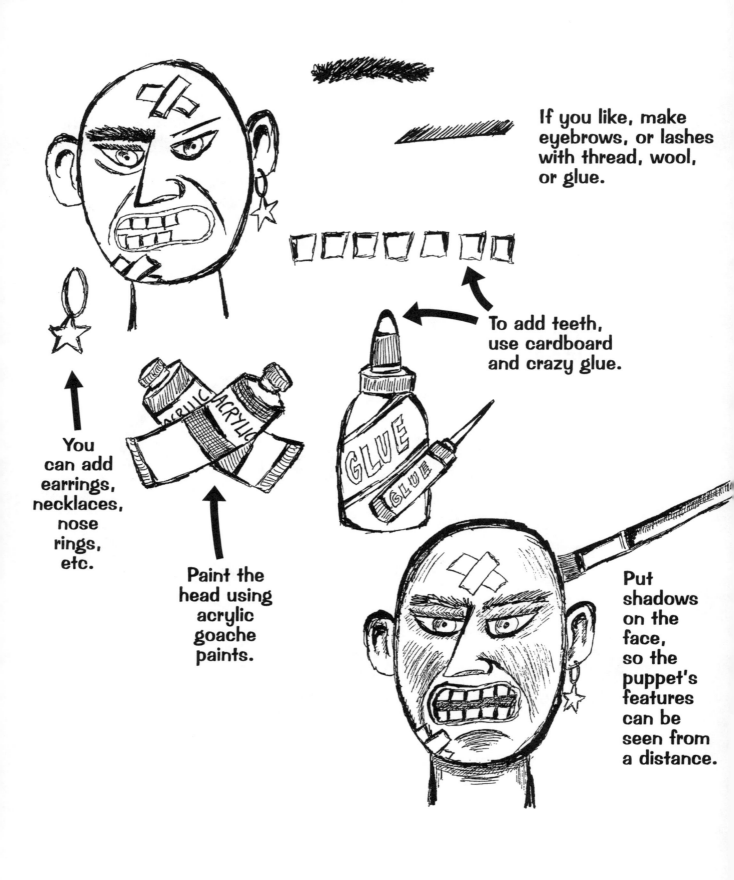

If you like, make eyebrows, or lashes with thread, wool, or glue.

To add teeth, use cardboard and crazy glue.

GLUE
GLUE

You can add earrings, necklaces, nose rings, etc.

Paint the head using acrylic goache paints.

ACRYLIC
ACRYLIC

Put shadows on the face, so the puppet's features can be seen from a distance.

For hair, use wool.

Sew the strands
of wool together.

Cut the strands
into a fringe.

Comb the
hair to make
it fluffy.

Use white glue
to attach the
hair to the
head.

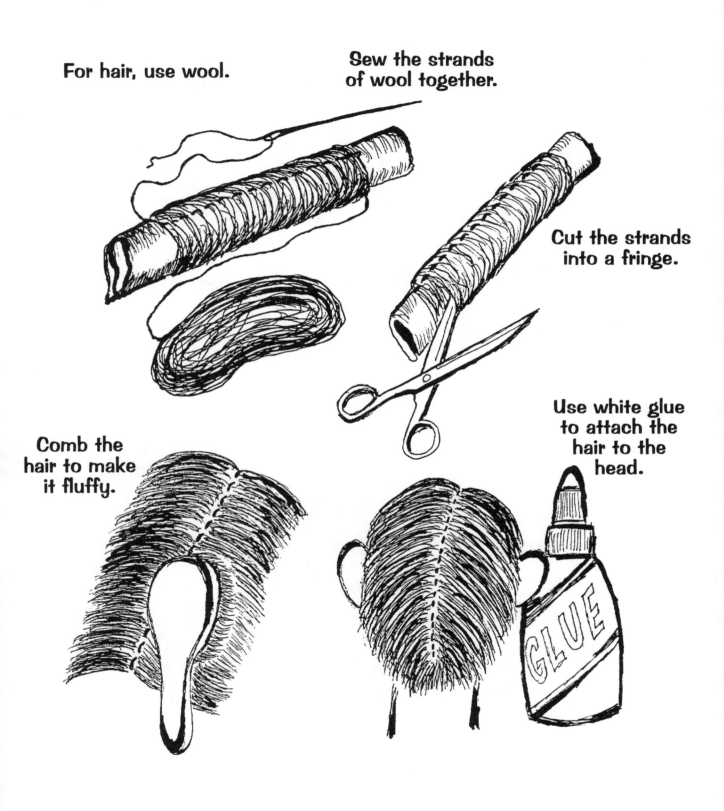

GLUE

...Or glue separate strands onto the hair.

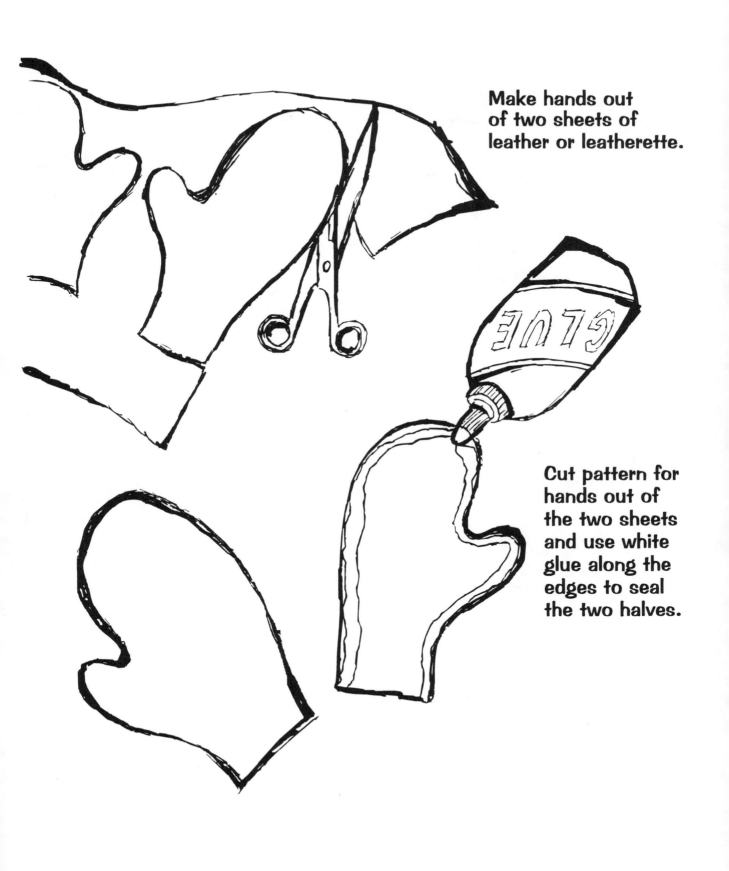

Make hands out
of two sheets of
leather or leatherette.

Cut pattern for
hands out of
the two sheets
and use white
glue along the
edges to seal
the two halves.

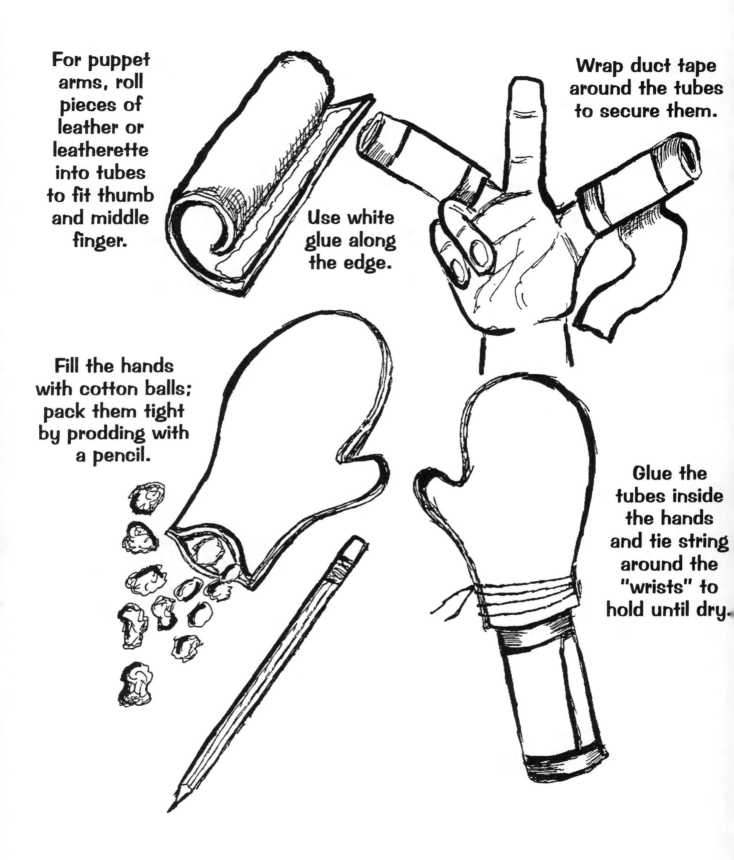

For puppet arms, roll pieces of leather or leatherette into tubes to fit thumb and middle finger.

Use white glue along the edge.

Wrap duct tape around the tubes to secure them.

Fill the hands with cotton balls; pack them tight by prodding with a pencil.

Glue the tubes inside the hands and tie string around the "wrists" to hold until dry.

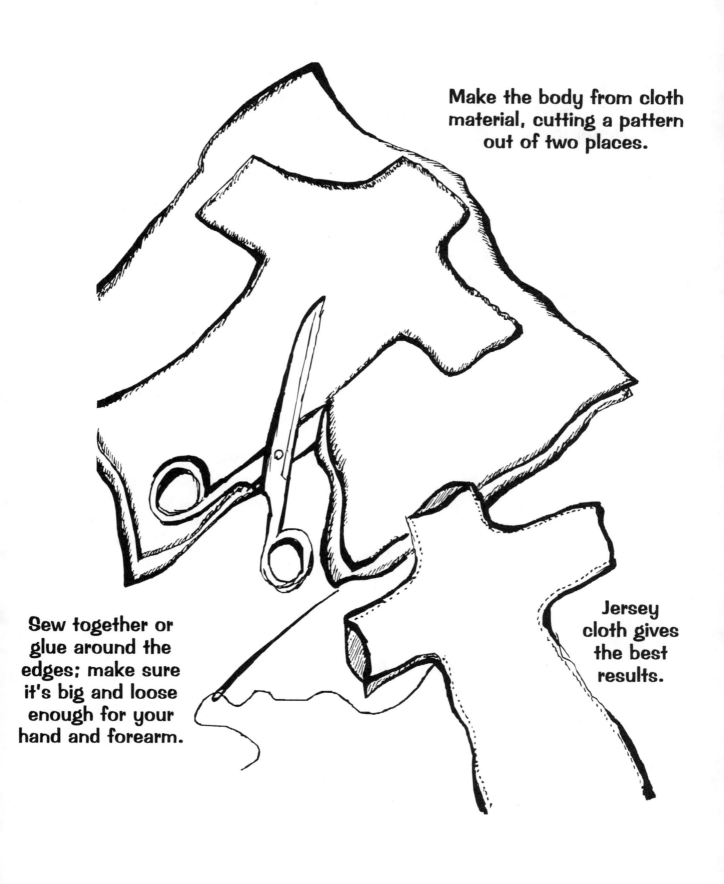

Make the body from cloth material, cutting a pattern out of two places.

Sew together or glue around the edges; make sure it's big and loose enough for your hand and forearm.

Jersey cloth gives the best results.

Using acrylic gouache, paint the hands the same color as the face...

Then paint lines to represent fingers.

Use white glue to fix the neck inside the collar.

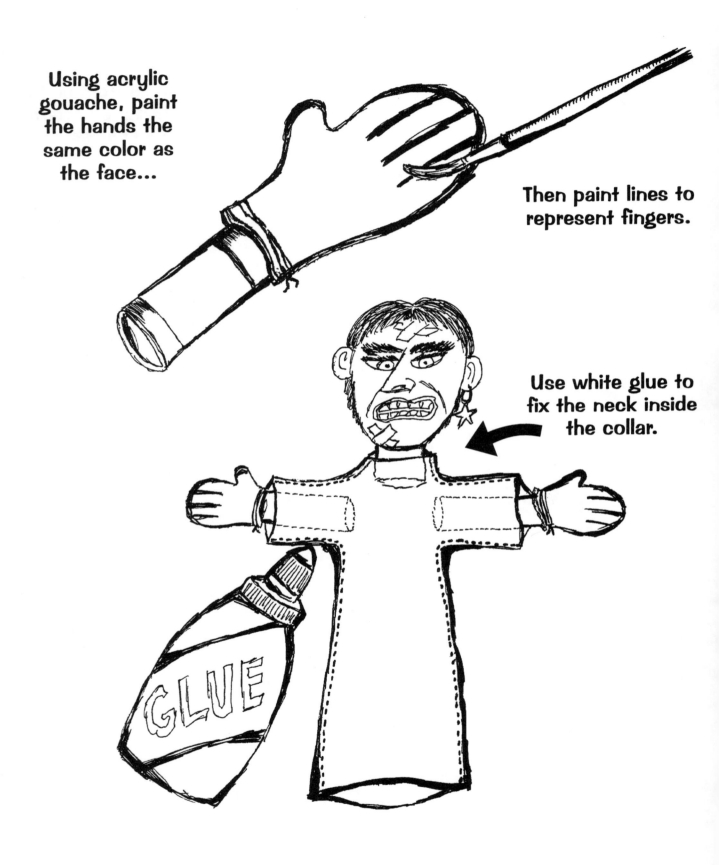

The body must cover your hand and arm loosely.

Tie some string around the neck and wrists while glue dries.

Make sure thumbs are pointing up when gluing hands to sleeves.

When all the glue is dry, try the puppet to see if it's easy to handle.

Then use material from old clothes to make the puppet's clothes. Sew a cloth pad on the body to give it girth.

Make the clothes roomy. Remember that your hand and arm must fit easily inside the puppet.

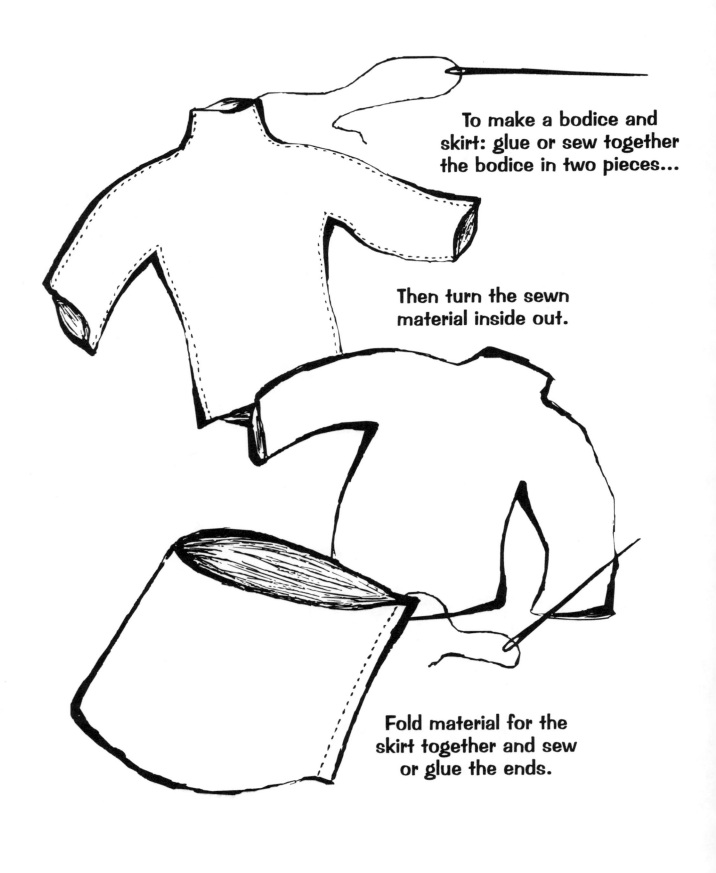

To make a bodice and skirt: glue or sew together the bodice in two pieces...

Then turn the sewn material inside out.

Fold material for the skirt together and sew or glue the ends.

Pleat the skirt until it fits the puppet's waist.

Dressing the puppet: glue the bodice onto the puppet's body at the neck and wrists.

Add lace, ribbons, etc., as it fits the puppet's character.

Sew the bodice to the skirt.

Shirt and pants: glue or sew together the shirt in two pieces then turn inside out.

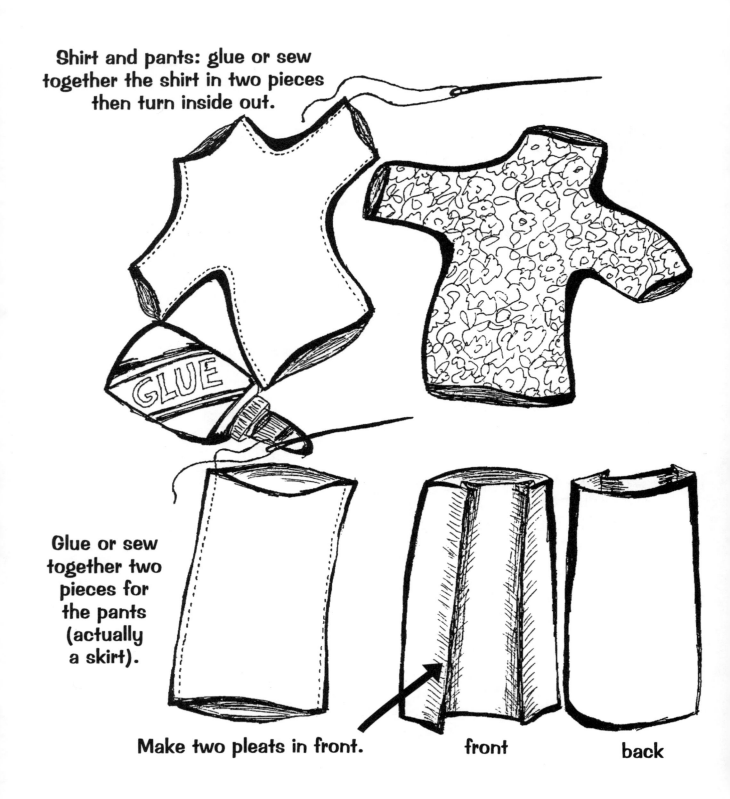

Glue or sew together two pieces for the pants (actually a skirt).

Make two pleats in front.   front   back

Glue the shirts to the body at the neck and wrists.

Sew the pants on the puppets body. Put shirttails inside or outside the pants.

MAKING THE STAGE

The hard way: build a simple portable wood frame screen, for use in classrooms, meeting rooms, or outdoors.

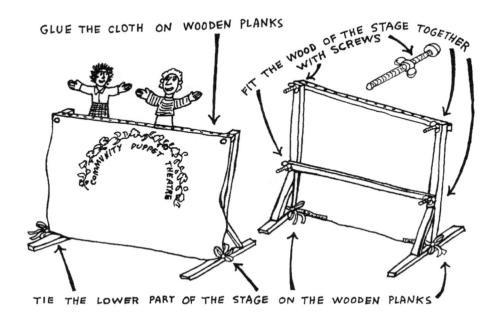

GLUE THE CLOTH ON WOODEN PLANKS

FIT THE WOOD OF THE STAGE TOGETHER WITH SCREWS

COMMUNITY PUPPET THEATRE

TIE THE LOWER PART OF THE STAGE ON THE WOODEN PLANKS

The easy way: just use a sheet draped over some clothesline.

Making Scenery

While scenery is never necessary when using puppets in popular education, sometimes participants want to use some in their skits.

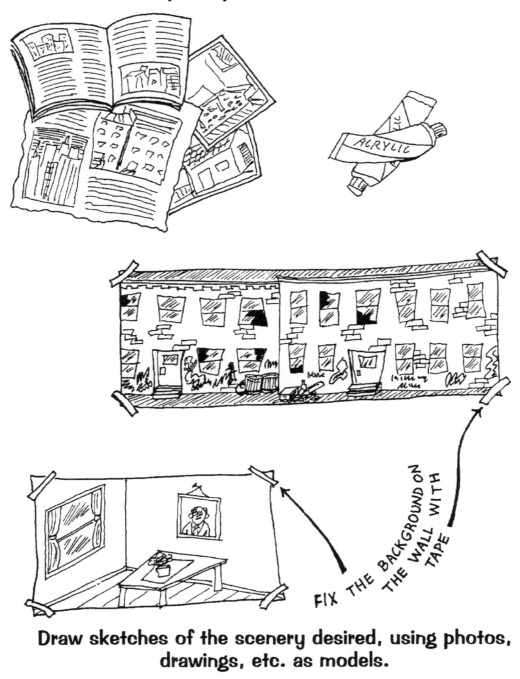

FIX THE BACKGROUND ON THE WALL WITH TAPE

Draw sketches of the scenery desired, using photos, drawings, etc. as models.

Draw and paint the background on a cloth using acrylic paints.

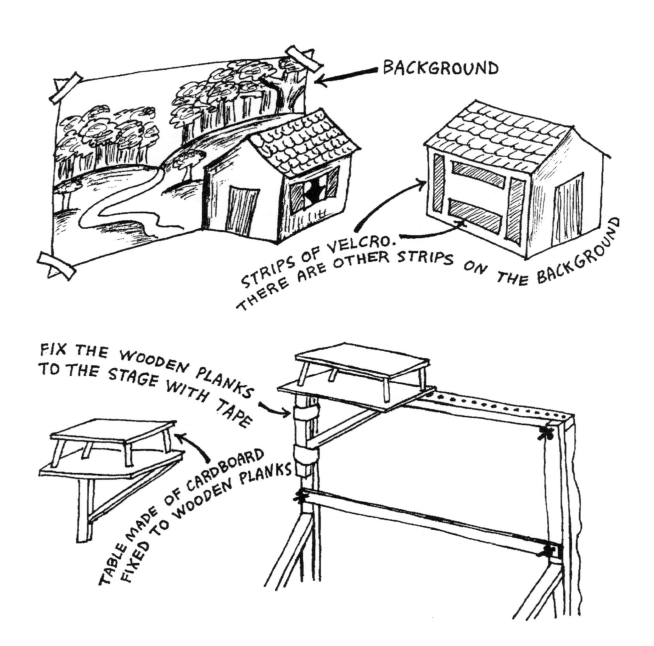

BACKGROUND

STRIPS OF VELCRO. THERE ARE OTHER STRIPS ON THE BACKGROUND

FIX THE WOODEN PLANKS TO THE STAGE WITH TAPE

TABLE MADE OF CARDBOARD FIXED TO WOODEN PLANKS

Participants can also make props that can be fixed to the backdrop with velcro or perched on to a wooden frame behind the stage.

DEVELOPING THE STORIES

It's very easy to learn how to handle hand puppets. Anyone can do it. The participants can practice with the puppets, developing the stories in a few hours.

The skits are presented to small audiences, made up of people from the same social group for whom the work is targeted. Stories are further developed and perfected as they are performed, when the puppets discuss the story's problems with the audiences. Some of the best ideas are born this way.

Producing Graphic Materials

Graphic materials are extremely important educational tools in popular education. An important principle of popular communication is the use of simple techniques and materials that are available to anyone, for the goal is to communicate with the people in their own language, not to do a slick, polished job. Use illustrated charts, leaflets, and comic book stories in all workshops and courses.

Newsletters and posters are also extremely important tools for organizing activities in unions, communities, and all kinds of grassroots organizations.

All educational materials should include illustrations (photos, drawings, graphs, etc.), the more the better; modest amounts of text; short, simple sentences. Language and illustrations used should be appropriate to the culture of the target audience.

Other important points: Always remember to use careful research, accurate data, and concrete examples of the problems you are discussing. Your classes are not likely to care about abstractions; reason about concrete things, not abstract concepts. The materials have to be changed/corrected/perfected all the time, according to the practical results you achieve through them.

Before preparing the graphic material, answer the three questions:

1. **Who is the target audience?** [Discuss the class: their culture, way of life, immediate problems, what they think about the issues up for discussion, etc.]

2. **What is the objective of the material we want to produce?** [Possible answers: to inform about an immediate problem; to organize a movement to resolve a problem; to help people to understand the root causes of a problem, etc.]

3. **What is the best way to attain this objective?** [Ask in discussion: What are the best arguments to use with the target audience, considering what we know about their culture, their way of life, their way of thinking, their immediate problems? Is it best to start by focusing on an actual problem or an hypothetical one (based in actual experience)? Is it best to use a comic approach or a serious one?]

IMPORTANT:

The way to really know the characteristics of the target audience is to talk with individuals from this group, in an informal way, in the community where they live. It's not possible to really know any social group through traditional research methods.

The best way to produce graphic materials in popular education is with the participation of members of the target audience, when this is possible—when they have the necessary skills and the time to do it.

Organizers in Brazil produced a piece of popular communication in the form of a comic book story. They used the three questions to prepare the project:

- **Who is the target audience?**

A group of construction workers in Rio de Janeiro who are not union members.

Most arrived recently to the city, searching for a better life. Sixty percent of this group are illiterate and they know almost nothing about labor laws, union organizing, etc. They come from the Northeast region of Brazil and are used to a form of popular literature called *literatura de cordel*, a kind of illustrated booklet depicting folk tales, historical and political themes, etc. The illustrations in the stories are crude and straightforward.

- **What is the objective of the material we want to produce?**
- **To show the need for worker organization and the need to change the administration of the Construction Workers' Union; to inform about labor laws in Brazil.**
- **What is the best way to attain this objective?**
- **This story shows the stark reality of the construction workers' lives, starting with the death of a worker, a very common occurrence in Brazil.**

To underline the need to organize, the story shows the consequences of a workingman's death on his family. The details are very serious, but Brazilian workers have a fondness for black humor; they often like comic relief in a serious story.

GRAPHIC MATERIALS IN POPULAR EDUCATION

PICK THE MOST USEFUL GRAPHIC MATERIALS	KEEP THE OBJECTIVES IN MIND	FIND THE BEST WAYS TO USE GRAPHIC MATERIALS	WHAT TO AIM FOR
• Comic book stories	• Creating a code	• Courses, seminars, institutes	• Many illustrations cartoons, photos, drawings)
• Illustrated charts	• Information	• Organizing campaigns	• Language and illustrations suitable to the culture of the audience
• Posters	• Boosting critical con-sciousness	• Alternative media used by grassroots groups	• Careful research, accurate data
• News-letters	• Organizing		• Concrete examples for solving problems, not abstractions
• Drawings	• Mobilization		• Change/correct/perfect materials in response to the practical results you achieve through them

WHAT TO ASK WHEN PRODUCING GRAPHIC MATERIAL IN POPULAR EDUCATION

1. WHO IS THE TARGET AUDIENCE?

Can we describe their class position, their culture, their everyday problems, what they think about the issues being discussed?

2. WHAT ARE OUR GOALS IN PRODUCING THE GRAPHIC MATERIAL?

Do we want to inform people about an immediate problem in their everyday life? Organize a movement to resolve a problem? Help develop critical analysis of the roots of a problem?

3. WHAT IS THE BEST WAY TO REACH OUR GOALS?

What are the best arguments to use with the target audience, taking into consideration their culture, way of thinking, and immediate everyday problems? Is it best to pose questions based on a real situation or a fictional one based on real events? Is it best to use a comic or serious approach?

The materials have to be changed/corrected/improved all the time, based on the practical results of their application.

KEEP VERY CLEAR IN YOUR MIND THE PURPOSE AND OBJECTIVE OF THE MATERIALS TO BE PRODUCED. IF IT IS TO INFORM ABOUT AN ISSUE, YOU CAN WRITE BIGGER ARTICLES, BUT ALWAYS USE SIMPLE LANGUAGE WITH PLENTY OF PICTURES DRAWINGS, CHARTS. IF IT IS TO MOBILIZE, WRITE SHORT SENTENCES, IN VIVID LANGUAGE. APPEAL TO THE IMAGINATION OF THE PEOPLE. MAKE THEM SEE HOW THEIR HOPES COULD BE REALIZED BY WINNING THE FIGHT.

THE LANGUAGE YOU USE MUST ALWAYS BE THE SAME LANGUAGE, THE SAME EXPRESSIONS, THE SAME WORDS AS THE TARGET AUDIENCE. NEVER USE THE LANGUAGE OF INTELLECTUALS WITH THE WORKING CLASS, THE LANGUAGE OF WASPS WITH OTHER ETHNIC GROUPS, DATED EXPRESSIONS WITH YOUNG PEOPLE, ETC.

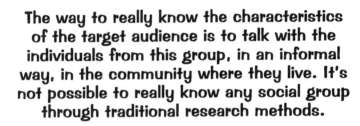

YOU HAVE TO UNDERSTAND THE CULTURE OF THE TARGET AUDIENCE, AND USE THE LANGUAGE AND EVEN THE ART STYLE MOST SUITABLE TO THIS AUDIENCE. GET TO KNOW AND USE THE POPULAR ART FORMS OF THE TARGET AUDIENCE.

The way to really know the characteristics of the target audience is to talk with the individuals from this group, in an informal way, in the community where they live. It's not possible to really know any social group through traditional research methods.

The best way to produce graphic materials in popular education is with the participation of members of the target audience, when this is possible—when they have the necessary skills and the time to do it.

THE PRODUCTION OF GRAPHIC MATERIALS IN POPULAR EDUCATION IS ALWAYS CONNECTED WITH THE GRASSROOTS MOVEMENTS. THE MATERIALS ARE PRODUCED BY PARTICIPANTS IN THE MOVEMENTS THEMSELVES, NOT BY OUTSIDE PROFESSIONALS

1. TO SEE the situation as the participants experience it

Ask the participants to describe the situation represented in the code.
Ask them to define the problems in the situation.
Make the link between the participants and the problems.

2. TO JUDGE the situation
ASK: Why did this happen?
What are the immediate causes and root causes (socioeconomic, political, cultural) of these problems?

3. TO ACT to change the situation
Discuss and carry out short term and long term action.

IMPORTANT:

The three steps (TO SEE, TO JUDGE, TO ACT) should be employed in the text of the graphic material you are producing. **This comic book story offers an example of how this can be done.**

TO SEE: This story shows the perils of the construction workers' life: no safety in the workplace, terrible work conditions, low wages. We also show the life of the construction workers' families, living in a slum, with no benefits, the children having to work, etc.

TO JUDGE: We show the immediate cause of this situation: the directors of the Construction Workers' Union have sold themselves to the companies' owners. We also show a deeper cause: the workers don't have enough power in Brazil to make laws that protect them, or to enforce the laws that already exist.

TO ACT: The story demonstrates how the construction workers can fight to defend their interests through organization. The suggested way to organize is to join the union and to fight for a strong union that really defends their interests.

The story starts with a common tragedy in the construction workers' life: a death in the workplace.

describing the terrible work conditions of the construction workers.

comic relief

The drawings are primitive, like the folk art in Brazil ("literatura de cordel").

Severino, like most construction workers in Brazil, doesn't know much about unions.

The immediate cause of the low salaries and bad work conditions of the construction workers.

comic relief (black humor)

Pedro talks about a way **TO ACT** to change the construction workers' situation.

The situation of the construction worker's family after his death...

Workers generally don't know much about labor laws in Brazil.

Information about the present laws...

Here we see the deeper cause of the construction workers problems: They have no political power.

Pedro explains the way to have power: Organization and action through the union.

The story ends with the ACTION of the construction workers defending their rights.

PRODUCING ILLUSTRATED CHARTS, FLYERS, POSTERS

As suggested in the preceding pages, a maximum of illustrations and a minimum of words is the best way to present information. Always try to use simple charts and graphs, comic illustrations, etc. The comic aspect catches the attention of almost all the target audiences.

In one workshop, a chart was needed to stimulate discussion about the low wages paid to Mexican workers in U.S. companies in Mexico (the "maquiladoras").

- Who is the target audience?
  Working class and middle class people.

- What is the objective of the material to be produced?
  To explain the principal reason why U.S. companies go to Mexico and other third world countries, and how this policy effects people's lives here.

- What is the best way to obtain this objective?
  A simple illustrated chart with data about the extra profit made by U.S. companies through paying lower salaries and no benefits to Mexican workers, and the resulting unemployment and increased federal budget deficit in the United States.

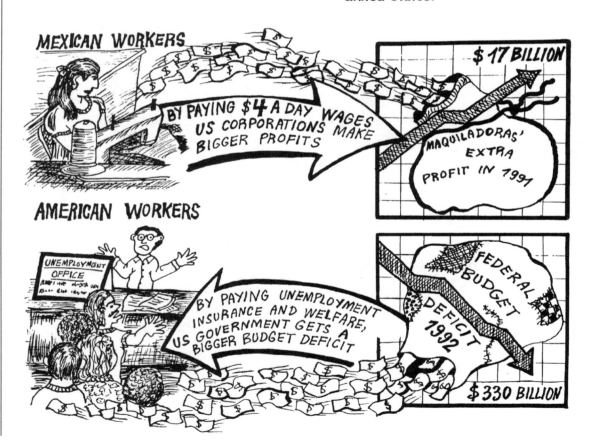

ONCE AGAIN THE THREE-STEP METHOD IS EMPLOYED TO ANALYZE THE CHART.

TO SEE

The chart shows the basic facts about the problem:

- low wages paid to the Mexican workers
- the extra profit made by the "maquiladoras" through this policy
- the U.S. federal budget deficit

TO JUDGE

Through the arrangement of the drawings, the data (wages, profits, budget deficit), and the arrows pointing in certain directions, the chart illustrates the causes of the "maquiladoras" policy of going to Mexico: more profit through lower labor costs, and the consequences here:

- unemployment and the socioeconomic problems it generates
- further growth of the budget deficit through decreased tax revenue from decreased production in the U.S.

TO ACT

The chart doesn't show any way to change this situation.
In this case the objective is to
INFORM and RAISE CRITICAL CONSCIOUSNESS.

Ultimately, however, this exercise must be reconnected to the overall goal of the project: identifying and applying a course of action to change the reality that generated the problem in the first place.

Part 5

POPULAR EDUCATION AND MULTICULTURALISM

Puppet workshop participants in an after-school program at the Community Arts Center (CAMBA) in Brooklyn, New York.

The idea that popular education methodology and techniques are suitable only for working people, or only in Latin America or some other third world setting, is mistaken. This same methodology and techniques can be used for all kinds of target audiences, in all kinds of situations: in high schools, universities, community centers, trade unions, grassroots organizations, etc., with people in all walks of life. Moreover, this methodology, with its basis in the dialogical approach, offers concrete solutions to the enormous problems of multicultural education in the United States.

In the Consortium for Worker Education, we worked with immigrants from many countries in ESL and GED classes using popular education methodology, and observed the differences in the level of participation and interest of the learners compared to classes using traditional methods.

The learners found they could discuss their problems, propose solutions, and learn much more quickly than they ever had in traditional educational settings.

For example, in an ESL class set up by the Teamsters union, cultural conflicts was used as the generative theme. There learners were Latin Americans, mostly relatives of union members. The class was divided into four groups, and each group developed a puppet skit about a cultural conflict they had experienced or heard about. Each group presented their skit to the class.

One of the most interesting stories told of a Latin woman unhappily married to a North American worker. When she told of her wish to get a divorce, her mother, a very traditional woman, told her that this was impossible and threatened to disown her. When asked how she could want a divorce, the daughter explained that her husband never took her out on weekends, not even for a walk in the park; he just stayed home watching ballgames on TV and drinking beer. He didn't like Latino food and never went to visit her relatives. At the mother's suggestion, the three got together to talk about their problems. The husband agreed to take his wife out dancing, to cook his own kind of food, even to visit her relatives.

When the skit was presented to the class, men and women alike said it was perfectly true that this kind of thing happens all the time in marriages of Latins and North Americans. A lively discussion about cultural differences developed. Starting from the stories, the educator was able to develop lessons about grammar, spelling, and other subjects, that held everyone's attention.

The same theme was used in ESL classes of Chinese students at the International Ladies Garment Workers Union, where the learners developed skits about conflicts between traditional parents and their U.S.-born children who don't want to learn Chinese, don't respect their traditions, etc. There was a discussion about the different cultures and customs, and the learners, usually very quiet in the classroom, broke into animated discussion of all the issues.

A similar result came from an ESL class of Haitians held by a public employees' union local. We began with a skit in which puppets of then-President Bush, a Haitian, and a North American businessman discussed U.S. policy on Haiti. The puppets interacted with the audience, covering all the possibilities, but soon the learners began to talk directly to "Bush" about his policy toward the ousted President Jean-Bertrand Aristide. The discussion was intense; the participants conversed with the puppet as if he were a real person.

Once again, the participants were divided into two groups to develop puppet skits on the generative theme of the situation in Haiti. The groups chose their characters, including a Tonton Macoute fascist, ex-Vice President "Baby Doc" Duvalier, an old woman, Nelson Mandela (as a leader of black people), and a businessman. The skits developed into a general discussion between the audience and the puppets, capped by a stirring speech for the return of Aristide, delivered by a woman through her puppet character.

What began as a class that day ended as an energetic rally by the participants. They were so absorbed that the action carried over, uninterrupted, into two other classes scheduled for later that day.

When a participant spoke up in defense of the Duvalier regimes, the language of the discussion shifted from English to Creole. The next day, two groups formed to prepare reports on the skits and discussion, using the blackboard. The educator corrected mistakes and gave lessons in grammar and spelling based on the reports. Once again the participants skipped their break and stayed late.

It should be pointed out that these examples, for all they accomplished in Freirean terms, failed to reach the third step: TO ACT. In each case, there lacked a follow-up by the educators to draw out paths of action the participants could take up to work for change around the issues they discussed.

Some action did result from a curriculum on cultural identity developed at El Puente Academy for Peace and Justice, a high school coordinated by a community organization in Brooklyn. The project began with teenagers drawing an "identity tree," along the same lines as the problem tree. The leaves and branches were marked with the elements of culture: the music the learners liked, the food they ate, their language, religion, traditions, etc. The trunk was the countries their families came from: mainly Latin America and the Caribbean. The roots were the original sources of their culture: indigenous African and European peoples.

This led to group research on the cultural legacies of the Taino people of precolonial Puerto Rico, as well as African slaves and European settlers. The groups developed multimedia presentations based on their research, using drawings, videos, music, skits, etc., to "share the wealth" of their studies with community people.

As these examples show, popular education techniques offer a unique approach to the problems of multicultural education in community settings. Through this methodology, learners can better understand their own origins, and the contrasts and conflicts that are an inevitable part of living in a society of increasingly diverse cultural traditions and experiences.

ESL students using puppets in a skit about Former President Aristide of Haiti.

THE BASICS
Practicing the Paulo Freire methodology in group settings

THIS IS THE KEY TO POPULAR EDUCATION IN PRACTICE!

IDENTIFY THE PROBLEMS

To identify the GENERATIVE THEMES the class will explore, GET ACQUAINTED with the participants.

Get to know their life and work settings.

Get the background and facts about the issues that affect them.

PRODUCE THE CODES

Create a concrete symbol (a drawing, a video, a photo, a puppet show, an audiotape, etc.) that represents the generative theme.

---

1. TO SEE the situation as the participants experience it

Ask the participants to describe the situation represented in the code.

Ask them to define the problems in the situation.

Make the link between the participants and the problems.

---

2. TO JUDGE the situation

ASK: Why did this happen?

What are the immediate causes and root causes (socioeconomic, political, cultural) of these problems?

---

3. TO ACT to change the situation

Discuss and carry out short term and long term action.

THE THREE BASIC STEPS ARE REPEATED OVER AND OVER, KEEPING UP WITH CHANGES IN THE SITUATION AS EXPERIENCED BY THE PARTICIPANTS.